GULF COAST CHRONICLES

Gulf Coast Chronicles

Remembering Sarasota's Past

Jeff LaHurd

Published by The History Press
18 Percy Street
Charleston, SC 29403
843.577.5971
www.historypress.net

Front Cover:
A whirl of light around the American Legion War Memorial at Five Points and east along upper Main Street. *Carmen Ramsey Collection. Sarasota County History Center*

Back Cover:
Dixie Graves, an Aquabelle at Sarasota's Sunshine Springs and Gardens, shops along Main Street. Sunshine Springs and Gardens was developed in 1955 by brothers Leonard and Charles Tanner in conjunction with the Lake Sarasota subdivision. *Mrs. J.C. Cash and Sam Montgomery.*

First published 2005

Manufactured in the United Kingdom

1-59629-029-3

Library of Congress Cataloging-in-Publication Data

LaHurd, Jeff.
Gulf Coast chronicles : remembering Sarasota's past / Jeff LaHurd.
p. cm.
ISBN 1-59629-029-3 (alk. paper)
1. Sarasota (Fla.)--History--20th century--Anecedotes. 2. Sarasota (Fla.)--Social life and customs--20th century--Anecedotes. 3. Sarasota (Fla.)--Biography--Anecedotes. I. Title.
F319.S35L327 2005
975.9'61--dc22
2005006946

This book was made possible through a grant from
The Sarasota Alliance for Historic Preservation.

Other Books by Jeff LaHurd

Quintessential Sarasota: Stories and Pictures from the 1920s to the 1950s
Sarasota: A Sentimental Journey in Vintage Images
Sarasota: Then and Now
Lido Casino: Lost Treasure on the Beach
Pitching Paradise During the Roaring 20s
A Passion for Plants: The Marie Selby Botanical Gardens

To my beautiful wife, Jennifer, for the happiest years of my life.

Contents

Acknowledgements

Gulf Coast Chronicles: Remembering Sarasota's Past is a compilation of the columns that I wrote for *Sarasota Magazine*, an article that I wrote for *SRQ Magazine*, "The Chicago Connection," an article on Ca' d'Zan that I wrote for *House and Home*, as well as some material that has never been published.

Without the ongoing support of *Sarasota Magazine*, neither this volume nor *Quintessential Sarasota*, and the other books that I have written, would have been possible. I am grateful to Pam Daniel, Dan Denton, Jimmy Dean and Ilene Denton for continuing my columns.

I owe a great deal to Pete Esthus for loaning me many of the photographs for this book and six others. Pete has been the keeper of the Sarasota flame for years, and his contribution to preserving our history cannot be overstated. Until he retired in 2004, his Sarasota Lock and Key shop on State Street was as much a museum of Sarasota's history as it was a business. To Nancy Wilkie, as always, my heartfelt thanks for being willing to help me with her editing skills and her advice about what sounds right and what does not.

For more than fifteen years I have been haunting the Sarasota County History Center, formerly the Sarasota County Archives, and I want to thank the always helpful staff there for their assistance and patience: Dave Baber, general manager; Ann Shank, historian; Lorrie Muldowney, preservationist; Mark Smith, archivist; and Dan Hughes, archeologist.

This book was made possible in part by a grant from the Sarasota Alliance for Historic Preservation, whose ongoing fight to preserve what we have left of our past in Sarasota should be appreciated by old-timers and newcomers alike. I thank the board members: David Jennings, president; Debra Flynt-Garrett, vice president; Lorrie Muldowney, vice president; Kafi Benz, newsletter editor; Joyce Waterbury, secretary; and Sandy Slaminko, Wilson Stiles, Chris Wenzel, Don Smally, Kittie Kelly, Harvey Hoglund, Judy Schomaker and Jesse White.

I received information for this book from the Sarasota *Herald-Tribune*, the *Sarasota Times*, the *News*, the *Sarasota Journal* and the *Sarasota Sun*; also from *The Story of Sarasota*, by Karl H. Grismer, Paschal and Paschal Publishers, 1977; *Sarasota Origins*, published by the Historical Society of Sarasota County, 1988; *Ringling: The*

The Sarasota Brass Band marches proudly along upper Main Street, carrying the Stars and Stripes in this 1918 photograph. Note the "Welcome Buddies" sign painted on the street to greet returning doughboys who had gone over there to battle the Kaiser's army in 1917. The flagpole was erected at the center of Five Points in their honor. In 1928, the American Legion War Memorial would be dedicated at this site, where it would remain until 1954. Another honor for the returning servicemen was the renaming of Main Street, east from Orange Avenue, as Victory Avenue and the planting of oak trees along the way, one for each Sarasota soldier. *Sarasota County History Center*

Florida Years, 1911–1936, by David C. Weeks, University Press of Florida, 1993; *The Circus Kings: Our Ringling Family Story*, by Henry Ringling North and Alden Hatch, Doubleday and Company, 1960; *Buckets and Brawn, The History of Sarasota and Its Fire Department*, by Wayne A. Welsh, 1993; *From Shield To Star*, by Robert M. Snell printed by Coastal Printing, 1999; and Roger V. Flory's Sarasota Visitors' Guides. I conducted interviews with Lillian Burns, Rudy Bundy, Frank Conrad, Art Goldberg and Joyce Price. I received information from correspondence between John Ringling and Owen Burns, provided to me by Lillian Burns.

Introduction

SARASOTA WASN'T ALWAYS LIKE IT is today, not by a long shot. It was better. For one thing, the community had a sense of its identity. We were unique—and we knew it. Landmark buildings, whether the Mediterranean Revival or Spanish Mission designs of the 1920s, the Art Moderne of the '30s or the modern, trendsetting Sarasota School of Architecture homes and buildings of the '40s and '50s, set us apart. There was no mistaking Sarasota for Clearwater, Largo, or St. Petersburg.

This is no longer true. Today, many of our most prominent buildings, rising up as quickly as space can be found to shoehorn them in, are seen in every large city in the state—unimaginative high-rises embellished with various doodad add-ons. By contrast, there was only one El Vernona Hotel, Mira Mar Hotel, ACL Depot and Lido Casino. Later, spurned on by local school board president Phil Hiss, architects from what came to be known internationally as the Sarasota School of Architecture—such as Victor Lundy, who gave us such singular buildings as the "butterfly wing" addition to Alta Vista Elementary School; Paul Rudolph, the addition to Sarasota High School; Tim Seibert and Jack West, the beach pavilions; and Carl Abbot, the Summerhouse Restaurant—cast the international spotlight on Sarasota. The dorms at New College were designed by the great architect I.M. Pei.

Another element that made Sarasota such an attractive place to live were the many and varied amenities this truly small community offered. The countywide population of permanent residents in 1955 numbered less than thirty thousand. There were less than twenty thousand in the city. It's difficult for newcomers to imagine what it must have been like to have lived in Sarasota when there were so few people to share space with. Those lucky souls and their visiting friends and relations were offered a world-class art museum, a renowned art school, a symphony orchestra, a professional stock company, an amateur theatre, a major league baseball team for spring training and a colony of artists, writers and architects of international renown. Add to the mix the winter headquarters of the Ringling Brothers and Barnum and Bailey Circus, the top attraction in the state, plus a potpourri of smaller tourist attractions: the Sarasota Jungle Gardens, Texas Jim's Reptile Farm, Horn's Cars of Yesterday, the Circus Hall of Fame, the Museum of the Circus, Ca' d'Zan, the Glass Blowers and a myriad of sporting and recreational opportunities from lawn bowling, to golf, to fishing, to trapshooting.

The undeveloped out-islands were pristine tropical paradises within sight of the mainland but seemingly far away and offered miles of superlative undeveloped beaches to stroll.

It's understandable that many longtime residents bemoan today's unbridled growth, often coupled with the destruction of the very places that we were proudest of and enjoyed the most. Add to the discontent six- and seven-lane highways clogged with traffic, water restrictions, out-of-scale buildings, particularly downtown, and a frenetic pace.

Whatever "planning" has been involved in the recent growth spurt has obviously been developer oriented, with the protection of landmark buildings not high on the agenda. When the El Vernona aka the John Ringling Hotel/John Ringling Towers was razed in 1998 despite the vociferous opposition of concerned citizens, a representative of the Crowne Plaza hotel chain told this author that his group could not believe that Sarasota would let such a significant landmark go.

What remains of yesterday's Sarasota are mostly our memories.

No exact dates mark the beginning and end of what we fondly remember here as the good old days. However, the fifty-year time period between the land boom of the 1920s and the misguided demolition of the Lido Casino in February 1969 encompasses most of it.

Interestingly, the joy of those idyllic days crosses all age groups. Whether you were a child in 1955 and spent your Saturdays at the Ritz Theatre or, as a young adult, cruised the Smack or went to the casino or, as an adult, dined at the Plaza, yesterday's version of Sarasota is a happy but bittersweet memory. In a commentary written for the Sarasota *Herald-Tribune* on December 19, 2004, renowned architect Edward J. "Tim" Seibert, FAIA, recalled his feelings about today's Sarasota: "I experienced a sense of loss and disorientation in that same neighborhood [First Street] a few days ago, when I walked down to see the new bus station, and suddenly knew how much I wanted the Plaza Restaurant back…There comes a sense of loss that sneaks up when you least expect it, and the lump in my throat and shortness of breath surprised me. There are more and more encounters in Sarasota that bring on this sense of loss for those of us who have spent our lives here."

There can be no doubt that today's Sarasota is "all grown up." But for many of us the recent unbridled growth spurt underscores the expression that more is less. Fifteen years have swept past since I tried to capture the best of what made up yesterday's Sarasota in *Quintessential Sarasota: Stories and Pictures from the 1920s to the 1950s*. The success of that book opened a door for me that led to five other books, a video, numerous articles about Sarasota's unique history and, most recently, a second career at the Sarasota County History Center as a history specialist.

That book struck a nostalgic cord with longtime residents, engendering pleasant memories of days gone by. I hope this book will too.

An Unhappy New Year

PITY OUR POOR SCOTTISH COLONISTS. Their New Year's Eve of 1885 should have been a joyous celebration of a new beginning, an adventurous opportunity to start 1886 with a prosperous new life in the New World.

The group had left hearth and kin behind for an arduous ocean crossing to what they had been told was a modern community on the tropical Gulf Coast of Florida. Scotland was in the throes of a financial depression, and brochures and newspaper accounts of Sara Sota painted an idyllic picture. The Florida Mortgage and Investment Company boasted of a "wonderful new town in the most beautiful section…small but very modern…where the land was fertile, the weather magnificent, where bumper crops of oranges and vegetables were assured." It was to be the pot of gold at the end of their rainbow.

Skeptics were won over by the investment company's stellar board of directors, which included prominent Scottish gentry, among them a relative of the Archbishop of Canterbury. This, they could rest assured, was no fly-by-night organization.

For one hundred pounds sterling, each family purchased a town lot in Sara Sota and a forty-acre estate outside of town, the site of which would be determined by a drawing. They made the necessary arrangements to leave their homeland, selling most of their belongings, and approximately seventy men, women and children (including some families from England) packed their most cherished possessions, bid farewell to family and friends and, on the night of November 25, 1885, boarded the 440-foot ship *Furnesia* for the long voyage. They called themselves the Ormiston Colony, after the home of Sir John Gillespie, one of the investment company's founders.

The scene at dockside was very emotional. Whatever ambivalence the Scots must have felt about leaving was surely magnified by the sadness of the departure. Nellie Lawrie, one of the children on the journey, later wrote that everyone was weeping as they sang the old Scottish song "Will ye no come back again / Better loved ye ne-er will be." By the time the lyrics "We'll meet again soon ither night, for the days of Auld Lang Syne" were sung, very few could get the words out. Tears were flowing.

The *Furnesia* steamed away from the lights of Glasgow and into the darkness toward New York (thanks to a broken piston, two stormy weeks away), then to

The John Browning family and some newly made friends in a photo taken at Cedar Point in 1886. *Sarasota County History Center*

Fernandina on Florida's east coast; next the colonists traveled by rail ("two streaks of rust") to Cedar Key and finally made their way to the side-wheel steamer *Gov. Safford*, which would bring them to their promised land.

During the stopover at Cedar Key, the first inkling of trouble surfaced. The anxious group learned that lumber for their portable houses had not been delivered. Fearing the worst, they stayed on through Christmas, and when they could no longer stand the anticipation, they boarded the steamer for the final leg of their journey.

On December 28, 1885 the boat navigated slowly into beautiful Sarasota Bay. It was late in the afternoon, and from the deck, staring across the azure water toward the shore, the passengers saw mangroves, scrubland and a few dilapidated buildings. Slowly they realized that Sara Sota, the modern town, existed only in the imaginations of pamphlet writers and as lines on a town plat.

A few pioneer settlers had gathered at the foot of the bay to greet the colonists and help unload their belongings. The newcomers disembarked onto two planks of wood extending from the shoreline, near where Marina Jack stands today. Until lumber finally began arriving, the bewildered colonists had to sleep under hastily erected canvas tents or bunk with locals. Some stayed in an old frame building.

Their unhappiness was pervasive. These were middle- and upper-middle-class families who had nothing in their backgrounds to prepare them for the wilderness that was Sarasota. Their "estates" were often far from the downtown area—some were ten miles away or more through thick forests—and the backbreaking labor involved in laying out streets and building and farming on primitive land was more than most could contend with. To make matters worse, temperatures fell to record lows, and one bitter cold day, snow actually fell. Freezing and miserable with disappointment, many soon fell sick.

Colonist Alex Browning summed up the feelings of the disheartened group in a memoir he drafted in 1932: "Of course there was much discontent, being dumped, like this, in a wild country, without houses to live in, tired and hungry, one can imagine what it was like. Families grouped around their mothers, while their fathers were trying to find out where they were going to live."

For New Year's Eve, the colonists banded together at the largest of the tents to "celebrate" by singing and playing whatever musical instruments they had brought.

After a few months, most of the colonists had had quite enough and moved on. Some returned to Scotland while others settled in more established American towns. A few died in Sarasota. One of those who stayed, John Browning (Alex's father), and his family helped to build Sarasota after the Florida Mortgage and Investment Company sent J. Hamilton Gillespie to revive the effort. Browning's descendants still make Sarasota their home.

In 1985 a citywide celebration commemorated the centennial of the colonists' landing. And while there will probably be no further fanfare about the group until another milestone year comes around, give them a thought New Year's Eve when you sing "Auld Lang Syne."

A Sarasota Romance

FOR MOST, THE STORY OF Bird Key extends back to the late 1950s, when Arthur V. Davis's Arvida Corporation bought the holdings of John Ringling and set upon the task of redefining Sarasota. Through a massive dredge-and-fill operation, the key was enlarged to accommodate 291 waterfront and 220 off-water lots. Bird Key was transformed, and to this day it continues to be a real estate agent's delight and remains one of Sarasota's premier addresses.

Sales began in 1960 with hoopla reminiscent of the land boom of the Roaring Twenties. Lots were offered for between nine thousand and thirty-two thousand dollars. Incentives for agents to sell, sell, sell included prizes of a twenty-seven-foot Chris-Craft Constellation cabin cruiser and a new Lincoln Continental.

But there is another story about Bird Key that very few know. It's a romantic tale of hope and heartbreak, and it began fifty years before Arvida discovered Sarasota's development potential.

This story began on a sunny afternoon in 1910. Mrs. Davie Lindsay Worcester, who was visiting from Cincinnati, took a launch with six friends to Bird Key, still a virginal paradise not connected to the mainland. The tiny island was only fourteen acres in those days and barely broke the surface of the water. But it was stunningly beautiful, filled with palm trees, brightly colored seashells, and the myriad of birds that flocked there for food and rest.

Mrs. Worcester was a woman of means and a singularly gentle lady whose reputation was forged on acts of kindness. As one of her friends put it, she was "a woman of great heart [who] loved intensely all that was beautiful in nature and humanity." She served on so many charitable boards that her hometown considered her the "greatest woman philanthropist [they] had ever known."

She came to Sarasota after an illness, hoping to relax and recoup in the salubrious climate. The beauty of Bird Key on that day so many years ago awed her. She wrote her husband, Thomas, one of the most vivid descriptions of Sarasota's beauty ever penned.

Choosing her words as carefully as a painter chooses colors from a palette, she wrote: "The shore was laden with shells…so beautiful I could not pick them, dear, at first. I felt that my heart would burst on that shell-bestrewn shore. With thousands of palms soaring toward the clouds; at our feet the Gulf of Mexico washing up,

New Edzell Castle, built by Thomas Worcester for his loving wife, Davie. *Sarasota County History Center*

restless, to our toe tips, and scattered, scattered everywhere…all beautiful toys, as it were; not given stingily or grudgingly but five, ten feet deep, perhaps; scattered like beautiful flowers so far as color and form was concerned, on that white sand, until you felt you could not tell the dear Father enough how grateful you were."

Thomas Worcester, described by a contemporary as "a courteous and pleasing gentleman…full of genuine romance" for his wife and anxious about her frail health, was moved by the description. They had been married for thirty-six years and he loved her dearly. In her letter she wrote that she longed for him to share her joy and added, "This is what I want for my old age…Oh! Words cannot paint the scene, imagination cannot conceive of such grandeur."

In 1911, Thomas bought Bird Key from the state and set about fulfilling his wife's wish. Sand from the bay bottom was dredged to increase the key's size. Davie, thrilled that her dream was about to come true, designed much of the home that she named New Edzell, in honor of her family's ancestral estate in Scotland.

The Worcesters' mansion took nearly three years to complete. At a cost of one hundred thousand dollars, it was lavishly furnished and outfitted with such amenities as electric lighting (practically a first in Sarasota) and acetylene gas. From the opposite shore it was said to glow with startling radiance; and as it was still not connected to the mainland, their launch, *Dido* (Mrs. Worcester's pet name), ferried the Worcesters and their friends back and forth.

Interior of the Worcester mansion. *Sarasota County History Center*

Sadly, on October 14, 1912, before her home was totally completed, Davie Worcester, who had never fully regained her health, unexpectedly died on Bird Key. She was brought back to the mainland on the *Dido* and taken to Cincinnati for a funeral service and then to Kentucky, where she was interred. Mr. Worcester, now a grieving husband, carried on with the project, and in 1914 New Edzell Castle was ready for a bittersweet housewarming. The *Sarasota Sun* reminded its readers that Davie was responsible for its design and called the mansion "a Tribute to the Genius of a Talented American Woman."

At a time when Sarasota was barely more than a fishing village, the home was a showcase. When parties were given, the guest list and the evening's goings-on were glowingly described in the local paper. One such soiree, headlined "Musical Across the Bay," was praised in the flowery prose of the day: "The harmony and beautiful strains from their instruments pealed throughout the entire mansion grounds to the utmost pleasure of all the guests." When the evening was over and the guests were transported back to shore, the paper noted, "As the yacht slipped away into the moonlight waters of the bay the many lights on shore winked and winked again, 'good night, come again.'"

John Ringling purchased Bird Key in the early 1920s and connected it to the mainland. He hoped that New Edzell Castle would serve as the winter White House for President Warren G. Harding, helping to advertise his development, Ringling Isles, and boost sales there. He named the streets on adjoining Lido Key in honor of American presidents. Ringling was quoted in the Sarasota *Herald* as saying that Harding "displayed all the enthusiasm of a big boy over his contemplated vacation in Sarasota...He had his desk covered with photographs of the Zalophus [Ringling's yacht]...and he seemed to be looking forward to his sojourn on it as a haven of rest.But when Harding died before the plan could be realized, Ringling's sister, Ida Ringling North, moved in and lived at New Edzell until she passed away in 1950.

Unfortunately, New Edzell Castle did not figure into Arvida's plans for Bird Key. Among the selling points was a $250,000 Bahamian-style yacht club, which was built on the site of Mrs. Worcester's dream house. As has happened so often in Sarasota, there was little effort to save the home for its historic import, and it was razed. Today, not even a historic marker exists on Bird Key to remind us of Davie and Thomas Worcester and what was to have been their retirement paradise. When you pass Bird Key, give a thought to the Worcesters, whose appreciation for beauty and love for each other led them to settle there.

Pioneers of Publishing

When newspaper man Cornelius Van Santvoord Wilson and his wife, Rose, arrived in Sarasota in 1899 after publishing the *Manatee County Advocate*, there was precious little here to suggest anything but a dubious future for them, their enterprise or the community.

In those days Sarasota was just a minor part of Manatee County, a sparsely populated village that was difficult to reach and offered only the barest necessities. Downtown had a livery, a blacksmith shop, a few homes, two boardinghouses and the DeSoto Hotel, which was usually vacant and looked older than its years. Livestock wandered freely. The bay front was littered with fishing shacks, fishing nets and whatever trash and garbage had washed in. Old photographs of early settlers document the harsh realities of their lives; the day-to-day battle to survive is clearly etched on their stoic faces.

But the old black-and-white photos fail to convey the area's intrinsic beauty. That beauty convinced Wilson, a justice of the peace known affectionately as "the Judge," to believe in Sarasota's potential for growth. On June 1, 1899 the Wilsons published the first edition of the *Sarasota Times*, "Devoted to the west coast of Manatee County." (When Sarasota broke away from Manatee, the newspaper was renamed the *Sarasota County Times*.)

The original printing plant was set up in a humble wooden building on the north side of lower Main Street, and the newspaper began as an oversized, four-page weekly produced on a hand press from hand-set type. Advertisements, the lifeblood of every newspaper, were meager at first; Wilson's personal savings and his earnings from selling real estate supplemented the venture. The paper sold for a subscription rate of one dollar per year.

The Wilsons were progressives who vigorously pushed for the growth and improvement of Sarasota. Rose championed the right of women to vote (she became the first Sarasota woman to register) and supported educational programs for Sarasota's children. She was also a charter member of the Town Improvement Society, which did much to beautify the downtown. Later, she would push for the building of the Tamiami Trail, and when the chamber of commerce was formed, she was elected to the board of governors.

For his part, C.V.S. Wilson believed that Sarasota's future lay not with cattle and fishing but with winter tourism. He editorialized about the need to

Home of the *Sarasota Times*, circa the early 1900s, when it was located on lower Main Street. *Sarasota County History Center*

improve Sarasota's infrastructure, and his newspaper campaigned for Sarasota to be incorporated into a town. He preached of the importance of advertising Sarasota's virtues. "All Hotels on the Manatee River are filled with Northern visitors," he wrote. "Here in Sarasota our hotels are empty. The reason is simple: we do not advertise. What Sarasota needs more than anything is a Board of Trade or Chamber of Commerce that will concentrate on telling the nation of our superb attractions."

He recognized the importance of offering recreation to draw newcomers and backed the effort to develop a local brass band. "There is nothing that gives so much snap and go to a town as a brass band," he wrote. "Let's have a band and keep abreast of the times." (The band was soon formed, and over the years it regularly entertained locals and snowbirds and was often present at the train station to welcome important personages.)

By 1910, the watershed year in which socialite Bertha Honore Palmer came here for a look-see, the paper's advertising had increased as more businesses had opened. Revenue was bolstered by an endless array of patent medicines that promised to cure all maladies. For instance, B.B.B. (Botanical Blood Balm) relieved practically every ailment by "purifying the blood." And at twenty-five cents a box, Dr. Schultz's Liver Tablets provided "a sure cure for Biliusness, Constipation and Torpid Bowel." They were sugarcoated and pleasant to take.

Although the Wilsons' newspaper printed the news of the state, nation and world, it was first and foremost community oriented. The comings and goings of its citizens were regularly reported. ("Grandmother Rogers has returned to her home in Warthering Springs." "Mr. W. Chappell and Mr. J.F. Spencer have been spending some time at Wimauma, where they are erecting a comfortable two-story home for Rev. H.H. Norris.") New arrivals to Sarasota's hotels and boardinghouses were listed, along with their hometowns and occupations. ("The yacht, *Merry McB*, belonging to A.C. Cobb, a hotel man, visited Sarasota last week.") Under the "Local Affairs" column were such tidbits as "Mr. Owen Burns has placed an order with D.W. Walker for a 25 ft. pleasure launch, to be built as soon as possible." Citizens were reminded that "C.W. Maus of Bradentown will be down this week to lead the services at the Presbyterian Church Sunday."

Deaths were reported with great dignity, as when F.B. Hagan passed away in 1914: "Much of his life has been spent in serving the public, having held many positions of honor and profit. Yet he was never accused, not even suspicioned of any act of dishonor or discredit to his unsullied reputation. His only fault—if he had faults—was his failure to properly appreciate his own worth and merit."

There were no photographs or cartoons in the paper's early years, but jokes were printed. "The gentleman at the foot of the stairs called up to his wife. 'I forgot whether you told me t' have two drinks and come home at 11, or 11 drinks and come home at 2.'"

Wilson wrote his last editorial on September 10, 1910. He told his readers of his illness and recognized the assistance of Rose. "For twelve years she has stood side by side with me in the publication of this journal," he wrote. "[It] is a credit to me and my paper that her name will be placed at the head of the editorial column…of the *Sarasota Times*." He ended, "Now, with life's duties finished and only awaiting the call to pass 'over the River' I lay down my pen and pencil. Put aside my stick and rule, vacate the editorial chair and walk out of the sanctum with honor unsullied, aged seventy-three. Farewell." He died on September 28, 1910. Five years later, the *Sarasota Times* was almost burned out in the great Sarasota fire of 1915. But volunteers, led by Rose, managed to beat back the flames and save the presses. The paper never missed an issue.

For thirteen years after the Judge's death, until the beginning of 1923 when Sarasota was on the cusp of the phenomenal real estate boom, Rose carried on. The paper grew to twelve pages, with a circulation of two thousand readers. Sarasota was rapidly changing into a modern town, drawing the newcomers that the Judge and Rose had envisioned so many years earlier. (When Andrew McAnsh, the builder of the Mira Mar Apartments, Hotel, and Auditorium, arrived in town, he was met at the train station by the brass band the Judge had lobbied for.)

In 1923, Rose sold the *Times* to two local businessmen, who then sold it to L.D. Reagin. Reagin moved the plant into a Mediterranean Revival building on today's First Street just off U.S. 41 (the building is currently being renovated) and continued publishing until the paper became a casualty of the Great Depression.

In her final column, "The Ties That Bind," Rose thanked her loyal readers for their support, saying that she was selling "to those who were prepared to enter the field and give the town a better newspaper service than we could." She ended, "Now that larger plans speak of a greater Sarasota there are none who feel a greater interest and pride than those who in the pioneer days caught the vision and paved the way." Rose died in 1964, her and her husband's role in Sarasota's success unknown to most of the hundreds of thousands who have followed them here.

The Pioneer Hotelier

For most Sarasota residents and visitors, Higel means no more than the name of Higel Avenue, the street that runs through Siesta Key. But during the era just before the Florida land boom of the 1920s accelerated our growth, Harry L. Higel, the man for whom the street was named, was a progressive dynamo, pushing the community toward its future. He managed to envision a backwoods, difficult-to-reach frontier settlement as a resort destination for wealthy snowbirds.

The Higel family first moved to Venice from Philadelphia in 1884. Harry came to Sarasota a few years later. The Scottish colony had already failed, and Higel purchased the dock the Scots had built at the foot of lower Main Street and a general store from the Florida Mortgage and Investment Company. He also sold real estate for the company's agent, J. Hamilton Gillespie, and became the area's first gasoline and kerosene dealer.

As the community inched slowly forward, Higel went into politics, served five terms as a member of the town and city council and was mayor for three terms. He fought hard for Sarasota to incorporate into a town. In short order, he became involved in the steamship industry, Sarasota's only regular link with the outside world, as an agent for a rich Tampa fish dealer and businessman named John Savarese. He later owned his own steamer, the *Vandalia*.

Then the focus of Higel's attention shifted to Sarasota Key, known today as Siesta Key. It was on the north end that he and two associates developed Siesta on the Gulf.

In those days Siesta was truly a remote tropical island, reachable only by boat. But it was so beautiful with its sugar sand beaches and vivid gulf that Higel was certain if he could get the word out and offer a place to stay, it could become a popular winter resort. As he put it, Siesta "was being largely developed along lines that appeal to the 'well-to-do,' who wish to leave the snows…and get down here for five or six months of continuous good weather."

Higel, along with E.M. Arbogast of West Virginia and Captain Louis Roberts, platted Siesta in 1907, and in a massive dredge-and-fill operation dug out canals and formed Bayou Louise, Bayou Hanson and Bayou Nettie. In 1913 he opened bathhouses for the day-trippers who came to Siesta by boat for swimming, picnics and fishing, offering refreshments and promising that "life lines, safety guards and all preventives of accident will be provided."

Harry L. Higel, tireless Sarasota booster and developer of Siesta Key. *Sarasota County History Center*

In a 1915 brochure, "Siesta on the Gulf," Higel wrote that Siesta was a "Place to Rest…Have Peace and Comfort." "Think of it! Living on a tropical island on Sarasota Bay where one can bathe in the waters of the Gulf of Mexico, hunt, fish, motor and enjoy life the year around." Testimonials praised the key's beauty, its desirability as a winter retreat, the bountiful fishing, even its potential for growing "a wide range of vegetables for shipping to marketing centers at a winter period when they have a monopoly on demand." J. Louis Houle was quoted in the brochure: "You should take a run down here and get cooled off. There is a really delightful, cool summer climate here along the Gulf Coast." And local real estate man I.R. Burns added, "Its location, its pureness of air and all other good qualities, which space forbids to mention, assure good and profitable investments to those who buy and not a better location for homes can be found anywhere."

Lots on the island were offered for two hundred dollars and up, with the E.A. Cumming Company giving terms of twenty-five dollars cash down and five dollars per month, with no interest for the first year. Those were pre-bridge prices, and advertisements assured that Siesta lots going for five hundred dollars would be worth five thousand within three years.

Siesta Key's crowning glory was the Higelhurst Hotel.

Higel had it built on Big Pass, perfect for bay and gulf views and a spectacular spot for fishermen. Two stories tall, with columns all around and a large screened porch on the second floor, it opened in 1915, with Higel ferrying two hundred celebratory guests to and from the mainland on one of his boats.

The Higelhurst Hotel, the hallmark of Higel's Siesta Key. *Sarasota County History Center*

The *Sarasota Times* reported that the ex-mayor was all smiles as he greeted his guests and offered them refreshments, dancing and card games. The *Times* added, "It proved his progressive spirit which dominates Sarasota's former mayor. Mr. Higel was preaching optimism and he backed up his faith in the future by planning a hotel."

Rooms rented for $2.50 per night, offering hot and cold running water, large baths and gas and electric lights. A large fireplace accentuated the ground floor, which featured large sitting rooms and a dining room that could comfortably sit 150 people. The eleven bedrooms were "splendidly furnished."

Higel appealed to sportsmen. Pictures of the hotel frequently showcased fishermen displaying their day's catch; one showed seven tarpon and a five-hundred-pound shark brought in by a hotel guest in four hours. Another displayed five hundred pounds of kingfish, caught in three hours by three guests. For swimmers the hotel sat less than fifty feet from the white sand beach.

The Higelhurst was truly one of Higel's greatest achievements. But within two years, just before the Siesta Bridge was officially opened, the hotel burned to the ground. "FLAMES LIGHT UP THE SKY," the *Times* headlined. Higel's son, Gordon Higel (later postmaster of Sarasota), recalled, "I remember the morning it burned. He went out and I went out with him, and he had me by the hand and we went to the seawall [on Gulf Stream Avenue]. There (in the distance) was a dream that he had accomplished and here all of a sudden it's gone. And I can see him now. I looked up at him and tears were just coming down his cheeks. I was nine years old."

Although Higel vowed to rebuild, he never did. But he continued to work hard for Sarasota and his beloved Siesta Key. With the bridge to Siesta nearing completion, he took out a large advertisement in the *Sarasota Times*: "SIESTA ON THE KEY BOOMING!" He recalled an earlier prediction: "In 1907 I...predicted Siesta was destined to be the best, high-class location in Florida...MY PREDICTION HAS COME TRUE."

Higel did not live long enough to fully enjoy the fruits of his labors. On January 7, 1921, his body was discovered in the middle of the road, his head and face so badly battered that he was not recognizable. He was driven to Dr. Halton's office on the mainland, barely alive. As there was no hospital in Sarasota, Dr. Halton cleaned his wounds and stabilized him as best he could and had him taken to Bradentown. Higel did not recover. He was fifty-four years old and left behind his wife, Gertrude, and three children.

Rube Allyn, the former editor and publisher of the *Sarasota Sun* and publisher of the *Florida Fisherman*, was arrested on circumstantial evidence and jailed in Bradentown for his safety. (Historian Karl Grismer wrote that he might have been lynched otherwise.) A grand jury was convened and decided there was not enough evidence to hold him for trial, and he was released sixty-one days later. A one-thousand-dollar reward was offered for the murderer, but no one else was ever arrested.

Sarasotans showed their appreciation for Higel's service to the community by turning out in force for his burial at Rosemary Cemetery. The *Times* reported that one of the largest processions ever known in Sarasota paid tribute at the grave and reminded that Higel was "a firm believer in Sarasota; and much of its early development as well as that of later years was due to his untiring activity in its behalf."

Into the 1950s and '60s, Siesta retained much of the vivid beauty and flavor of its early years. It had become an inspirational haven for writers and artists, who strolled the secluded white sand beaches and found camaraderie at the nearby Beach and Crescent Clubs, where everyone knew everyone else. As late as 1954, there were only five thousand permanent residents on the key.

No one can say what Harry Higel would think of the modern version of his tropical retreat. He could never have imagined Siesta as it is today. One thing is certain: he could not promise that there was nothing to "interfere or obstruct our view of the sun setting behind the waters of our great and grand Gulf of Mexico."

The Dynamic Duo of Sarasota's Development

The original John Ringling Causeway and the bridge that John Ringling bankrolled to open Lido Key to the public in 1926 is long gone, but a drive to St. Armand's with its wide, palm-lined boulevards festooned with antique statues, upscale shops, restaurants and hallmark circle attest to his vision and to the hard work of him and his associate, Owen Burns.

When Sarasota fell into the economic doldrums of the late 1920s, Ringling's announcement in 1927 that he was moving the winter headquarters of the world-famous Ringling Brothers and Barnum & Bailey Circus here was a financial and psychological boost and became a major tourist draw for more than thirty years. Thereafter, Sarasota was known around the world as the Circus City, home of the Greatest Show on Earth.

Ringling did not move to Sarasota with a view toward becoming its patron saint. Initially, he was a seasonal visitor, drawn here by the beauty, peace and quiet. Like so many who followed, he chose Sarasota as an escape from the madding crowd, a winter haven in which to rest and relax before striking out with the circus for another long and arduous tour.

But it did not take long for him to see the area's potential for profit in real estate—and not simply in the buying and selling of parcels of property. Ringling lived, to use a word popular today, large. He was grandiose in his vision. The once-poor son of a small-town harness maker, who had become one of the richest men in the country, saw through wide eyes. By the time he moved to Sarasota in 1912, he was enjoying a life of yachts, Rolls-Royces, private railway cars, important friends and connections with oodles of money. Although the great Ringling Brothers and Barnum and Bailey Circus was the foundation of his empire, he also scored in oil, railway lines and banking and was a partner in Madison Square Garden. The development of Sarasota was another, albeit spectacular, area of endeavor to apply his business acumen and reap the rewards surly due to a visionary capitalist willing to take a calculated risk. When lightning struck in the form of the Florida land boom in the early '20s, Ringling was financially flush and poised.

At this juncture, it was Ringling's good luck to meet and conduct a great deal of business with Owen Burns, another capitalist who had come to Sarasota by way of Chicago on the heels of Bertha Palmer in 1910.

Standing at the entrance to the El Vernona Hotel (left to right), E.T. McAdams, Owen Burns's accountant, U.S. Attorney General Daugherty, and Owen Burns, 1927. *Courtesy of Lillian Burns*

Burns purchased the holdings of the Florida Mortgage and Investment Company, the failed Scottish land syndicate, for a reported thirty-five thousand dollars and at once became the owner of approximately 75 percent of what would become the city of Sarasota. At the time the prospect for Sarasota's success was dubious.

An inventory of the town's primary assets in the early years makes for a quick read: the Belle Haven Hotel on Gulf Stream Avenue (in desperate need of repair), the pier at the foot of lower Main Street, some stores and inns along the main thoroughfare (a dirt road), a livery, a watering trough at the center of Five Points, a few buildings, some homes and the Halton Sanitarium/Hotel, which accommodated the Palmers on their first visit. Amenities to ease the daily struggle of everyday life here were few.

Livestock freely wandered the streets of the primitive community; the bay washed up to the shoreline, the downtown area's front yard, and deposited abandoned boat hulls, seaweed, dead fish and miscellaneous debris. Raw sewage drained into Sarasota Bay.

Farmers and ranchers lived on the outskirts of town and, like the fishermen whose nets and fishing shacks littered the bay front, they were not interested in changing the status quo in order to be attractive to wealthy northern visitors.

In spite of what Sarasota lacked at this time and as unpromising as its future might have appeared, its beauty was truly captivating and its potential was as immediately obvious to Burns, as it had been to Mrs. Palmer and would be to John Ringling and his brother, Charles.

Burns quickly established himself in the community. He aligned with the progressive element and during the next few years formed several companies to conduct his business affairs, and later some of the business of John Ringling: Burns Dock and Commercial Company, Burns Realty Company, Burns Dredging Company, Burns Transportation Company and Burns Supply Company.

At city council meetings, he spearheaded a renewed effort to clean up the bay front at Gulf Stream Avenue and build a seawall there to enhance the downtown area—the community's crown jewel. He also put forward the notion of installing street signs at all intersections, pushed for better roads and would back the break from Manatee County in 1921.

In 1911, Burns organized Sarasota's first locally owned bank, the Citizens Bank of Sarasota (later the First National Bank), and was elected the first president of the board of trade, the forerunner of the chamber of commerce. The whirlwind of his activities never ceased and would accelerate with his alliance with Ringling. Burns's civic endeavors included the reorganization of the Sarasota Yacht Club, helping to establish the Woman's Club and revamping the nine hole course that Gillespie had laid out, which his company "placed in first class condition adding greatly to the pleasure of our winter visitors."

In the years immediately preceding the Florida land boom, Burns and John Ringling formed a unique business association, with Burns often acting as Ringling's agent in Sarasota, especially during the lengthy periods of time that Ringling was away on circus business. Their relationship was sometimes contentious, sometimes tenuous, and ultimately it would end bitterly, but for a few heady years, the duo was the primary catalyst for transforming Sarasota into one of the most appealing resorts in Florida.

In almost all ways these two giants of Sarasota's early development were dissimilar. Ringling was flamboyant, gruff and as colorful as the circus he managed. He was used to the spotlight and enjoyed his celebrity. Some of his business dealings were, to be kind, imaginative, convoluted, even questionable. He traveled throughout the country, wheeling and dealing, borrowing from Peter to pay Paul, hiding assets when it suited him, exaggerating assets when it was necessary. His marriage to Mable, whom he truly loved, lasted more because of her understanding and forgiveness than his matrimonial diligence. His nephew, Henry North, termed it "Aunt Mable's loving acquiescence."

Burns, on the other hand, was a homebody, the quintessential husband and family man. He shunned the spotlight (pictures of him are difficult to find) and was above board in his business dealings. He was a proud Southern gentleman, a descendant of the War of 1812 hero Captain Otway Burns. His word was his bond; his handshake was as good as a signature on a contract.

Burns the businessman was totally focused on the success of Sarasota. From the time he arrived here, it became his life's work and he committed all his money and effort toward that goal. Whether he was working on one of his own projects

The great man himself, John Ringling, with his ever present cigar. *Sarasota County History Center*

or acting for Ringling, he was a hands-on supervisor. But despite the gargantuan amount of work for which he was responsible, he was home every evening with his wife, Vernona, and their five children for grace and dinner. (An incident related to me by Burns's daughter, Lillian, sums up Burns the family man. On the twenty-first birthday of his son, Leonard, Burns told him as he swept past to go out with friends for the evening, "You may be twenty-one and you may be a man, but you're never too old to kiss your father.") Both Lillian and her sister, Harriet Burns Strieff, remembered their father as "a very caring person, always there for us." He was devoted to Vernona, with whom he fell in love at first sight and married in 1912.

During Ringling's absences from Sarasota, he and Burns corresponded back and forth through letters and telegrams, always using the formal salutations "Dear Mr. Ringling" and "Dear Mr. Burns" and even "Dear Sir." Never "Dear Owen" or "Dear John."

Ringling could be demanding and Burns did his best to accommodate, which was not always easy. A telegram to Ringling from Burns dated September 20, 1922: "Dear Sir, Not receiving a reply to the three telegrams I sent you in California, I was obliged [to] cease operations." Earlier he had written to Ringling, "I wish to assure you that I am here to render you any service I can possibly do."

Ringling could not have found a more competent or conscientious person than Burns to oversee his interests in Sarasota. Not only was Burns a man of integrity, but he was an on-site, roll-up-the-sleeves supervisor. He did everything from counting the coconut seeds that would ultimately line the keys—"eight thousand eleven of them plus fifteen hundred and fifteen sprouted plants"—to being the point man in dealing with the myriad of problems, large and small, that were a daily part of diverse building projects that included bridges, homes, Ringling's mansion, apartments, bungalows, real estate and Burns's grand El Vernona Hotel.

At least on one occasion Ringling expressed his appreciation for Burns's efforts. In a letter dated April 3, 1923 Ringling closed by saying, "I assure you that I appreciate your help very much."

Back and forth the letters and telegrams flew, requesting money or offering progress reports, advice, orders, occasional congratulations and disappointment. They offer an interesting insight into how Sarasota evolved. Sadly, at the end of the boom—indeed, because of it—personal letters and telegrams were replaced with summonses, court orders and judgments. The tenuous relationship turned into bitter animosity and court battles.

One of the earlier Western Union telegrams, undated but probably sent to Ringling in 1922, regards the Sarasota City Council's wish to know whether Ringling would be interested in constructing a hotel or a hotel and recreational park in the three-hundred-thousand-dollar range for occupancy January 1, 1923. The city expressed a willingness to furnish light and water and waive taxes for a period of ten years. The only other proviso was that the park had to be open to the general public for three days a week in the winter and seven days in the summer. Burns ended by saying, "the council expected to accept the first satisfactory proposition along these lines." Ringling was not interested, a decision he probably later regretted. Andrew McAnsh took the offer and built the Mira Mar Apartments, Hotel and Auditorium, which signaled the beginning of the land boom here.

At the end of December 1922, a Burns letter to Ringling included a clipping of McAnsh's arrival to town—he was greeted as a hero, met at the train depot by a brass band—and told Ringling, "There is a very good feeling prevailing here and it looks as the town may go over the top this season."

Burns was involved in an ongoing campaign to buy up the south end of Longboat Key for Ringling to develop. On March 30, 1923 a three-page letter detailed his progress: 71 acres of the Woods property was purchased for $3,000; for the Edmondson property, the exact acreage was difficult to pinpoint but the price would be $4,500; the 34 acres of the Rodriguez property was going to be difficult to negotiate as "he won't sell for less than $200"; the Rorer property would go for $100 per acre for 32 acres. He told Ringling that the Palmers were going to sell their holdings "at much less than they paid for it." After these properties were bought, there would be only one 5-acre plot to finish the gulf front. Soon the south end of Longboat Key would be the setting for a grandiose Ringling project, the Ritz-Carlton Hotel—at least that was the plan.

Coconut palms would line the projected streets and boulevards of Lido Key, St. Armand's Key and Longboat Key, and Burns wrote Ringling that while the nuts and sprouted plants had arrived, there was a problem about the price. The captain of the boat that had brought them said the nuts were twelve cents apiece while the sprouted plants would go for one dollar each. Ringling wrote back, "If he thinks they are worth anything like $1.00 apiece you had better let him take them away ...he told me 25 cents or 30 cents. 10 cents apiece for the nuts."

On August 9, 1923 Ringling wrote from New York that Mrs. Ringling was planning a new house (Ca' d'Zan). Ringling sought Burns's advice regarding local architect Thomas Reed Martin.

The Ringlings had been meeting in New York with Dwight James Baum, who wanted to spend the winter in Florida for health reasons. Would Burns recommend Martin? Further, would he mind checking with Martin to see what type of "special arrangement he would make as it is going to be quite a pretentious house." Three days later Burns responded that he had spoken with Martin, who felt he "could do it justice." Burns said of Martin's capabilities, "He appears to have considerable artistic ability, is energetic and has done some very good work here." As to the special arrangement (of his salary), Martin would take a fee not to be greater than 5 percent of the cost. But Burns prudently left the choice to the Ringlings, saying that since they had interviewed Martin several times, "you would be in a better position to make that decision." Although Martin had drawn plans for the Ringlings, they chose Baum instead, and Burns's construction company would build Ca' d'Zan.

Ringling's advice to Burns regarding who should manage Burns's grand El Vernona Hotel, which opened with great fanfare in 1926, proved to be dubious. Ringling wrote to Burns on October 16, 1923, "Dear Mr. Burns, This will introduce you to Mr. H. Griswold a personal friend of mine who is going to Sarasota on business. He is one of our best hotel men and any courtesies shown him by yourself will be very much appreciated. Yours, John Ringling." Burns hired Griswold, a choice he would soon regret. According to Lillian Burns, Griswold skipped town without notice and without paying his lease, leaving Burns high and dry in the middle of the El Vernona's opening season.

With the opening of the Mira Mar Apartments and Hotel on Palm Avenue, the growth of Sarasota increased dramatically, and Ringling and Burns pushed forward with various projects. By 1926, Golden Gate Point was dredged and filled and lined with seedlings. So were the barrier islands, with Lido Key the site of Ringling Estates. The St. Armand's project was moving forward, and the Ritz-Carlton Hotel was going up. The John Ringling Causeway and Bridge was completed, as was Ca' d'Zan, and the construction of the John and Mable Ringling Museum would soon be under way. Also completed were Burns's projects: Burns Court, his building at Herald Square and his purchase of the Casabona apartment building, which he would rename the El Vernona Apartments.

Lido Key was opened to the general public on February 7, 1926, and sales of Ringling Estates were brisk. It was advertised that "Common Sense Prices Distinguish this Development," with waterfront homesites on the Gulf of Mexico priced at eight thousand dollars. Ringling hired the Czecho-Slovakian National Band for the celebration, and in his green Rolls–Royce, he led a parade of cars across the span. The Sarasota *Herald*, fanning local enthusiasm, called Lido Key a "tropical Utopia: of wide boulevards, canals, palm trees and alluring parkways." Thousands went across in cars or buses that left hourly from downtown. It was said that Ringling spent between $750,000 and $1,000,000 on the causeway and bridge, which was billed as "one of the greatest engineering accomplishments in the South."

In June 1927, Ringling gifted the bridge (and the headaches that went with it) to the city, prompting the Sarasota *Herald* to write, "There are no words adequate with which to express our appreciation for this wonderful donation…It will only be natural that beautiful homes and fine estates will be erected on the keys. And when this is done, Sarasota will be the cynosure of all America and the World." What may have been Roaring Twenties hyperbole proved to be prophetic.

By the end of 1926 the building frenzy was nearly over. The hurricane that ripped through Miami in September was the death knell to unbridled statewide speculation, and while Sarasota had enough momentum to continue forward, there was a decided slowdown; the end was near.

The downturn affected Ringling's ability to complete the Ritz-Carlton Hotel and directly led to the Ringling-Burns fallout. While Burns's El Vernona, which would soon be the grandest of the area hotels, was taking shape on Broadway Avenue amid much cheering and acclaim, Ringling's project slowed and stalled. His periodic promises to move forward notwithstanding, only the shell of the hotel, into which good money was thrown after bad, ever materialized. In May 1929, Burns, who owned a 25 percent share of Ringling Estates, Inc., from whence some of the good money came, sought an injunction to prevent Ringling "from manipulating the Sarasota Ritz-Carlton Hotel Company and the John Ringling Estates, Inc. to require the one to stand for the obligations of the other." Burns saw a goodly slice of his personal fortune being frittered away in an ill-advised attempt to revive Ringling's white elephant.

According to a newspaper account about the suit filed by Burns in the circuit court, when Burns ceased to be vice president of Ringling Estates in 1927, that corporation was flush with $3,706,400 worth of assets and only $5,989 in debts. Burns believed that Ringling, by mortgaging these assets, was involved in "a studied scheme…to cause John Ringling Estates to underwrite loans to the [Ritz-Carlton] hotel company," and ultimately confiscate the 25 percent interests that Burns held in John Ringling Estates.

December 1, 1930 was as bitter for Owen Burns as it was sweet for John Ringling. Under the headline "Ringling-Burns Troubles Compromised," the

Sarasota *Herald* reported that the suit filed by Burns had been dismissed, "and all charges of fraud had been retracted." Ringling was given clear title to all the disputed properties on St. Armand's, Lido Key and Longboat Key. Sadder for Burns, another article reported that the El Vernona Hotel had been sold to the Prudence Bond Company for $125,000. It is not difficult to imagine the angst that Burns must have felt at losing what was probably the most glamorous hotel ever constructed in Sarasota. Burns barely escaped personal bankruptcy.

A heavier blow landed when the El Vernona Hotel, named to honor his wife, was purchased for a fraction of its cost by John Ringling, who changed the name to the John Ringling Hotel.

While Burns was not the type of man to bring his business problems home, his daughters, Lillian and Harriet, who were children when the El Vernona was foreclosed, overheard enough adult conversation to agree that their father felt betrayed by Ringling and also by Sam Gumpertz, who would later turn on Ringling. Ever optimistic, Burns looked to the future. Although he had lost the majority of his properties and fortune in an effort to keep the El Vernona afloat, he began a new venture, producing guava jelly with the same enthusiasm that characterized his development days. He set up shop in the defunct *Sarasota Times* newspaper plant, a few steps across the street from his former office building and his splendid hotel, both ever present reminders of better days and the perfidy of former associates. He was not bitter. He had the love of his family to sustain him, a positive view of the future and an aura of self-confidence based upon his enormous accomplishments.

Lillian recalled that during the worst of the Depression, after he had lost his hotel, office building and most of his fortune, she found him sitting at his desk, tearing up some papers. "They were IOUs," she recalled. He told her that the notes were from those financially worse off than he. He advised her to never worship money, for it was only paper.

Owen Burns died unexpectedly at his home on August 27, 1937. He was sixty-eight years old, the owner of Tre-Ripe Citrus Guava Preserving Company. In his obituary the newspaper listed his major accomplishments and noted "he had been connected prominently with virtually every development in the city." Postmaster L.D. Reagin summed up Burns's work in Sarasota with this simple statement: "He was one of the leaders in making Sarasota what it is today."

The same could have been said of John Ringling, whose last years were characterized by business setbacks, hounding creditors, problems controlling the circus, a loveless second marriage and illness. Ringling died in New York on December 2, 1936. He was seventy years old.

Stormy Weather

THE DOWNSIDE OF LIFE IN the tropical paradise that is Florida includes the hurricanes that periodically roar through the state, leaving varying amounts of death and destruction behind; 2004 was a particularly devastating year, with four major storms.

And while Sarasota has been extremely lucky, other sections of the state have experienced catastrophic damage and loss of life. In the storm of 1928 it was reported that a tidal wave came out of Lake Okeechobee some five to ten feet high and cascaded across Pahokee, South Bay and Belle Glade, leaving approximately two thousand people dead. If that same storm occurred in today's vastly more populated state, the loss would be even more staggering.

The Labor Day storm that ravaged Key West in 1935 with winds estimated at more than two hundred miles per hour left four hundred dead and tore up the rail line that Henry Flagler built to connect the keys to Miami. Nightmare-sized waves swept homes off their foundations. An article in the Sarasota *Herald* illustrated the randomness of fate, telling of the Parker family: mother, father and eleven children who washed out to sea in their home and then washed back in again a mile away without injury. John Russell, on the other hand, lost sixty-eight of his seventy-nine relatives, including his wife and four children. Two hundred fifty-six World War I veterans who were working at government work camps along the keys died that horrible weekend.

After that hurricane, the U.S. Hurricane Service opened offices in Jacksonville, New Orleans and San Juan and increased coastal observations and weather advisories, using sophisticated weather equipment sent aloft in balloons.

Nearby storms included a fierce hurricane in 1846 that blew practically all the water out of Tampa Bay and left only four feet of water in the Manatee River. Two years later a storm hit Sarasota and pushed the gulf over the keys, blew down the Egmont Key lighthouse, broke ships apart and created New Pass.

The hurricane of 1921 was thought to have helped alter the course of Sarasota's history. It blew into the downtown bay front and destroyed the fishing huts, sea shanties, fish warehouses and old piers, taking away what some citizens felt were eyesores preventing suitable development. The estimated $150,000 storm damage was focused almost entirely in that section. The day after the storm, Mayor A.B.

Gulf Stream Avenue, littered by the hurricane of 1921. In the background, the Hover Arcade. *Sarasota County History Center*

Edwards issued a cleanup proclamation, and the rubble the progressives thought was holding Sarasota back as a resort town was hauled away.

Another history-altering storm produced the opposite effect, temporarily stopping Florida's growth. The hurricane that blew through Miami on September 18, 1926 crashed the Florida real estate boom, ending the speculative fever that was spiraling out of control. Hundreds perished, homes lost roofs, boats were dashed to bits and tidal waves washed over the Venetian Causeway. No loss of life was experienced in Sarasota or Bradenton, but each community suffered a million dollars in damage.

Former postmaster of Sarasota Gordon Higel remembered in a newspaper article that one of those most severely injured was "an eminent bootlegger," who in plying his wares strapped bottles of hooch to various parts of his body under baggy clothes. Before he could divest himself of his inventory, he was blown off a curb by the winds, cutting himself to the extent that he required one hundred stitches to close the wounds—but he needed no antiseptic to clean them!

A generation later, our luck held again when Hurricane Donna struck. It had been projected that its eye would move directly over Sarasota with winds to exceed one hundred miles per hour. Donna had already killed more than a hundred people in Puerto Rico, but before it reached us it changed direction and went inland at Fort Myers and across the state. An article by hurricane center director Dr. Neil Frank declared that if it had maintained its course, more than 150 miles of the Florida west coast from Fort Myers to Clearwater would have been devastated.

Hurricane parties are the upside to the big blows that Floridians contend with during the hurricane season. Copious amounts of booze are consumed by cooped-up residents marveling at the gusting winds and heavy rains, excited by the fury of Mother Nature. One downtown bar on lower Main Street was named the Hurricane Room for its storm parties. The newspaper reported that two babies were born at the height of Donna. What is not known is how many Sarasotans were conceived during that storm, but some forty-five-year-olds may be named in her honor.

Field of Dreams

FOR MORE THAN SEVEN DECADES, as a quiet community of a few thousand grew to today's bustling city, Payne Park remained one of the constants, a link to our past shared by each generation. Although the city recently completed grand new plans for the old park, to many of us it will always be synonymous with sunny spring afternoons, hot dogs and major league baseball.

Our field of dreams lacked the size and stature of a Yankee Stadium or Crosley Field, but from 1924 through the '80s, Payne Park hosted some of the greatest teams and the greatest players in baseball history. Four major league teams called it home: the New York Giants (1924–27), the Boston Red Sox (1933–58), the Los Angeles Dodgers (1959), and the Chicago White Sox from 1960 until March 30, 1988, when the last game was played there against the Texas Rangers. Baseball legends from "the Rajah" (Rogers Hornsby), to "the Splendid Stick" (Ted Williams), to "the Pudge" (Carlton Fisk) played at Payne Park, and so did hometown sluggers in Little League, Pony League, Babe Ruth League and various softball leagues.

The park was built between 1923 and 1924 on sixty acres of downtown land that Calvin and Martha Payne deeded to the city in the early '20s, stipulating only that it be for "a park, playground and kindred uses." At first the property was used for the county fair, and as was common in those days, volunteers pitched in during public work days to clear the land and erect the necessary buildings.

In 1924, a big league baseball diamond was fashioned on a portion of the property to induce the New York Giants, then baseball's hottest team, to come for spring training. Red clay was hauled in from Georgia for the infield. The city negotiated a deal with the Giants legendary manager John J. McGraw, "Little Napoleon," and hoped to receive reams of publicity from nationally syndicated reporters who accompanied the team. According to the *Sarasota Times*, the sportswriters would be happy to cooperate, "as Sarasota is a delightful relief after some of the bald headed villages in Texas where major league clubs trained last season." After the first spring training season ended, the *Times* noted that "Sarasota got more advertising in the last 60 days than in any similar period of its history. The town has really been put on the map." McGraw was said to be a real booster of Sarasota. As for the players, the Sarasota *Herald* wrote, "There is no finer, cleaner, example of American manhood today than the average ball player. He is

Payne Park, 1936, surrounded by a Tin Can Tourists convention. *Sarasota County History Center*

a gentleman, courteous, gracious and alert, keen minded and clear. It is a distinct pleasure to meet and to be associated with these fellows."

The team and the scribes were impressed with Sarasota but stayed for only four seasons. John J. applied his name and reputation to local real estate, with a subdivision named Pennant Park, north of Whitfield Estates. Gigantic ads with McGraw's picture ballyhooed it as "One of the Most Beautiful Bits of Homeland in the World." Its streets were to be named after baseball legends. As one ad put it, "There isn't a man who has ever been admitted to John J. McGraw's friendship who wouldn't walk across the brimstone pit on a rotten rail to save him." (Not mentioned was McGraw's dictatorial ways; he once said, "With my team I am an absolute czar. My men know it. I order plays and they obey. If they don't, I fire them." Nor was he averse to verbally abusing umpires, opponents, coaches and his own players.) One of his ads, "Watch That Man on Third!" advised, "THE MAN ON THIRD, the man who is going to steal a run on you, is the man who has already sent in his check for a reservation for a home-site in PENNANT PARK on Sarasota Bay." After the Florida real estate boom suddenly collapsed, and evidently a lot of "men on third" had sent checks, John J. decided it was prudent not to return to Sarasota and face investors.

The area adjacent to the ballpark was sometimes used as a site for the Tin Can Tourists' national conventions. Tin Canners were vagabonds who poked fun at their modest budgets by placing a tin can atop their radiators to symbolize the cans they dined from on their travels around the country. Many traveled in groups, and

Chicago White Sox manager Bill Veeck and friends at Payne Park. In the background, the Sarasota Terrace Hotel. *Sarasota County History Center*

they came to Sarasota by the thousands every year, much like the Air Streamers of today. Some of them liked Sarasota and stayed, and thus evolved Sarasota Mobile Home Park. In vain did critics, including the Paynes' grandson, Christy, point out that a trailer park was not what his grandparents had had in mind when they donated the land to the city.

In 1933, the Boston Red Sox organization brought big league baseball back to Sarasota, with the curse of the Bambino still, but not forevermore, haunting them. The Sox had been doing poorly until they got future Hall of Famer Joe Cronin to manage them in 1937. By 1938 the Sarasota Visitors' Guide bragged that Sarasota had the largest winter colony of baseball players in the world. In 1959, the Red Sox shocked the community by moving to Arizona. But the stadium was in top-notch condition and had no difficulty attracting another team. The Los Angeles Dodgers played here in 1959. In 1960, Sarasota welcomed Bill Veeck's Chicago White Sox, who soon bought the nearby Sarasota Terrace Hotel (now the County Administration Building) to accommodate the team. The White Sox remained our home team until 1997.

By the end of the 1980s, Payne Park seemed too small and too worn for the big leagues. Sarasota built the White Sox a modern facility, the Ed Smith

Stadium, on Seventeenth Street, and on November 1, 1990, demolition of the old stadium began.

The new Payne Park that has arisen in its place conforms to the wishes of Calvin and Martha Payne. The city and county cooperated on the park, which includes lighted tennis courts, a jogging trail and benches in an attractive, landscaped setting. There is also a skateboard area. At some future date, the city hopes to incorporate a memorial to the greats who once played baseball at Payne Park and to the Paynes themselves, who showed their love for Sarasota by giving its citizens a beautiful park.

The Kiwanis Club

On Armistice Day in 1922, practically all of Sarasota turned out for the parade celebrating the forth anniversary of the end of World War I. Old Glory flew throughout the city, and colorful red, white and blue bunting hung from the second floor of City Hall, stretched on the columns of the Watrous Hotel and was draped from the porch railing of the Belle Haven Inn. Long before the parade began, people lined Main Street, ready to wave their flags and cheer on the marchers.

Among those marching on this star-spangled day were a group of sixty-eight men who were about to present themselves to the community as the newly formed Kiwanis Club. Many had distinguished themselves in different parts of the country as doctors, lawyers, architects, bankers, developers and clergymen. They had been drawn to Sarasota for a number of different reasons but had in common a fervent belief in the town's future and the desire to push the community forward.

Smartly outfitted in white pants and shirts, dark ties and straw hats, they formed up directly behind the brass band in columns of three and marched proudly up lower Main Street toward the memorial flagpole at the center of Five Points.

In 1922, Sarasota gave little sign of the glamorous resort it was to become. Downtown had no fashionable hotels or upscale restaurants, Siesta Key was the only key linked by a bridge to the mainland and transportation to the area was mostly by boat and train. The roads were in deplorable condition.

But all of that was about to change. Sarasota was only a moment away from the biggest real estate boom and building spree in its history, and the members of the Kiwanis Club—"We Build" was their motto—were to be among the driving forces and the guiding lights.

After the parade, the men gathered around the flagpole for an official photograph. The club's early membership roster was a veritable who's who of Sarasota's history: John Hamilton Gillespie, A.B. Edwards, J.H. Lord, Owen Burns, Ralph Caples, Thomas Reed Martin, to name a few. Their fashionable homes and developments laid the foundation for today's modern city.

The members of the club were concerned about developing the spiritual health of the community as well as its economy, and they embarked on a variety of projects to this end.

They took a special interest in the youth of Sarasota. Frank Conrad, an active member since 1935, remembers the club's affiliation with the Boy Scouts, then

The newly formed Kiwanis Club of Sarasota posing on the front porch of the Bay Island Hotel, 1922. *Sarasota County History Center*

headquartered on Siesta Key. And he said that during the Depression, the Kiwanis Club set up a milk fund for school-age children, sent underprivileged children to camp and paid for the medical care of many needy youngsters.

Their major fund-raiser from the early 1920s to 1942 was an annual concert at the Mira Mar Auditorium. The featured soloist was always Verman Kimbrough, a Kiwanian who was also president of the Ringling School of Art, mayor of Sarasota and superintendent of the county school system. His son, Robert Kimbrough, is still an active Kiwanian.

The Kiwanis used the funds to help the elderly as well as the young. One of the club's biggest projects was building a haven for Sarasota's homeless senior citizens. They started the project after several Kiwanians investigated a house that was supposed to be caring for the elderly and found eight to ten men crowded in a room, hungry and covered with sores. The club combed the city for donations, and in 1948 the Sarasota Welfare Home welcomed its first guests. Situated on ten acres of beautiful pines and oaks, the facility had two dormitories, a dining room and a kitchen. Today, renamed the Pines of Sarasota and modernized, it has grown to become one of the finest nursing homes in the state and recently added an adult congregate living facility and adult and child day care.

This is the club's eighty-third year of service to Sarasota. The original club, now called the Downtown Kiwanis Club, has 150 members and has sponsored seven other Kiwanis Clubs in Sarasota. One of the newest, the Aktion club, is made up of developmentally disabled adults. Most live at the Children's Haven and Adult Center. As in any other Kiwanis Club, members elect officers, formulate an agenda for public service and sponsor a fund-raiser. The club's sponsor, Art Goldberg, who also helped to found the Boys and Girls Club in Sarasota, says that the Aktion club has allowed people who were formally dependent upon the community to experience the pride of contributing to it. The Aktion club idea was recently adopted by Kiwanis International.

Projects like this have made every one of the eight decades of membership rewarding, says Frank Conrad. "The Kiwanis has let me have an impact on Sarasota that I would not have had as an individual."

The County Courthouse

Sarasota has spent approximately six million dollars renovating this historic building, and the results are impressive. Revealed are many original architectural treasures long hidden under carpeting, above drop ceilings and behind paneling—thick, colorfully stenciled beams, marble floors, quaint glass skylights, heavy wooden doors and ornately carved wrought iron trim. Even the exterior has been repainted the original peachy shade so popular in Sarasota's 1920s-era buildings. The restored courthouse recalls a more genteel era, when citizens passed through screen doors rather than today's metal detectors and armed security guards.

The courthouse is one of the architectural gems that Dwight James Baum created in the Mediterranean Revival style that defined Sarasota and served as a symbol of the community's sophistication and bright future. Baum's buildings underscored Sarasota's arrival as a fashionable, upscale community; those that remain are among our most significant historic treasures, including Ca' d'Zan, Herald Square, the *Sarasota Times* building and the Belle Haven Apartments. (Perhaps Baum's greatest achievement, the El Vernona Hotel, later named the John Ringling Hotel, was demolished as the John Ringling Towers in 1998).

Baum already enjoyed a national reputation when John and Mable Ringling brought him to Sarasota to design Ca' d'Zan. "Each of his buildings here is unique," says David Baber, general manager of the Sarasota County History Center. "Ca' d'Zan, for example, has a Moorish flavor; the courthouse has Northern Italian influences and others are more Spanish oriented."

Sarasota needed a courthouse of its own after separating from Manatee County in 1921. For a short time, the seat of the newly formed Sarasota County was housed in the Hover Arcade at the foot of lower Main Street and shared space with City Hall. A temporary quarters was then built on Oak Street, but the need for a larger, more suitable building became obvious as Sarasota's growth started taking off. The city of Venice sought to place the county seat there and offered land and money toward the cost of construction. The local establishment, however, resided in Sarasota, and the current site east of town, on what was then called Victory Avenue, was chosen.

Baum was selected for the project in March 1925, the peak year of the local real estate boom. The site chosen was adjacent to the newly completed Sarasota

The Sarasota County Courthouse, 1959, in a picture taken from Main Street. *Sarasota County History Center*

Terrace Hotel and belonged to Charles Ringling, who sold the property to the county for a nominal fee. Stevenson and Cameron, with a bid of $366,426, won the contract for construction. Notable among the workers on the courthouse was Samuel Yellin, an internationally renowned wrought iron artist responsible for the Bok Tower in Lake Wales and the elaborate ironwork at Miami's Vizcaya, Henry Flagler's mansion. His unique craftsmanship, along with the terra-cotta ornamentation, enhances Baum's design.

There had been a holdup in the project for several months because the county could not get the materials needed for construction. The granite cornerstone, filled with documents pertaining to the county's history, was finally laid on May 13, 1926 with suitable fanfare and speeches. The Sarasota Masonic Lodge No. 141 F. and A.M. in full regalia was on hand. Judge Cary B. Fish told the crowd that the courthouse surpassed any on the west coast of Florida in architectural beauty and magnificence. He reminded the audience that the entire county worked together to make the dream a reality. While the children sung a hymn, the men in the crowd of hundreds took off their hats and bowed their heads.

The focal point of the courthouse is its campanile, or bell tower, situated between the building's two wings. The tower is closed off now, but once citizens could walk up poured-concrete steps to enjoy one of the loveliest views in all of Sarasota. Topped with yellow and blue tiles and surrounded with urns and numerous finials, the campanile was adopted as the county's logo and reinforces the reputation the courthouse has long enjoyed as one of the loveliest buildings of its type south of Washington, D.C.

The east wing was once the judicial center, the site of the sheriff's office, his upstairs living quarters, the jail and the courtroom. In those days, Sarasota was segregated, and black members of the community were relegated to a balcony in the courtroom.

The two-story wings are linked by a covered walkway. Clerk of Court Karen Rushing's office on the second floor of the west wing was once the commission chamber. Nowhere is the difference between today and yesterday more obvious than during the walk from the section of the courthouse that faces Ringling Boulevard into the second floor of the restored west wing. It's like passing through a time portal—cross over the threshold, and carpeting, fluorescent lights, drop ceilings and glass doors make way for terrazzo floors and marble walls, hanging lights and thick wooden doors.

Though most of the renovation is complete, some work remains to be done. For example, Baber hopes that a fountain that was once attached to the south side of the campanile will be replaced. But he admits there is no hope of replacing today's metal detectors and armed guards with the inviting screen doors of eras past.

Those Magic Elixirs

AH, THE GOOD OLD DAYS. No Food and Drug Administration to muck up science with silly tests and waiting periods. No truth-in-adverting requirements to diminish a product's appeal. In the good old days, if you had an illness, someone manufactured a cure. It was positively, absolutely guaranteed to work, and you didn't need to waste your doctor's time or take up space in a hospital bed to get it.

Advertisements in the *Sarasota Times* around 1915 touted the health-giving properties of tonics, elixirs, pills, potions and creams. Herbine, for instance, was a guaranteed cure-all for the many diseases associated with torpid liver. A large bottle cost fifty cents, a humble price for being able to "fully realize the Joy of Living."

Mother's medicine chest was bound to have baby's favorite tonic, White's Cream Vermifuge, "the best worm medicine offered to a suffering humanity, the permanent fixture of all households." Good stuff.

Skin problems? Mrs. N.E. Rowan received no succor from her physician. No sir. Her skin was as red as flannel and she felt weak all the time. Thank the Lord for Electric Bitters. After three bottles of this joy juice, Mrs. Rowan's skin cleared and she had enough energy to assist her husband in his store. (And cook, sew, clean house, put up preserves, do the marketing, launder clothes, beat the carpet and lube the Model T.)

Bad blood has long been a bane of American society. Before Geritol, druggists stocked Leonardi's Blood Elixir, "the Greatest Blood Medicine of the 20th Century." One testimonial told this story: "When all other remedies failed, Leonardi's cured me." This miracle in a bottle warded off rheumatism, catarrh, blood poison, scrofulous afflictions, ulcers, nervous debility and run-down condition, too.

And to make things even better, Badger's Pharmacy, Sarasota's "Store of the Town," promised to stand behind every product purchased. ("If at any time you buy anything from us that does not give you entire satisfaction, we'll consider it a favor if you tell us about it.")

For those inclined to be forgetful, listless and dull during the day, the time was nigh to crack open a bottle of Nyal's Iron Tonic Bitters, which encouraged blood and fed weakened tissues.

And how's your husband behaving? Been acting, well, not quite right? Send for a bottle of Dr. Hammond's nerve and brain pills, "A boon for weak

Advertisement for No-To-Bac, with the words of wisdom "Don't Tobacco Spit and Smoke Your Life Away." *Sarasota County History Center*

men." Six bottles were guaranteed to cure any disease for which they were intended—all those "thousand and one indescribable bad feelings." If the desire for the sinful pleasures of demon rum was one of his indescribable feelings, you could always administer the White Ribbon Secret Liquor Cure. Tasteless, odorless and colorless, this powder had the power to cure drunks without their knowledge. It could "reform the most abandoned drunkard." One could buy thirty treatments for $1.10. Just mix it in his morning coffee and dry away your tears, dearie.

Is your dear-heart's downfall tobacco? The poison weed habit could be conquered. For one dollar, ten thin dimes, Sears, Roebuck and Company, "the Cheapest Supply House on Earth," would send direct to your front door Sure Cure for the Tobacco Habit. It, too, dissolved in his coffee.

Now that the dear boy has sobered up and no longer reeks of smoke, is he focusing too much attention on that buxom little tart at the grocery store? Not to worry. The Princess Bust Developer came with a positive guarantee to enlarge any lady's bust by three to five inches. "If nature has not favored you," just send in $1.50—and stand back! As actor Joe E. Brown would have put it, "Wow!"

The health-giving benefits of exercise and wholesome food were not lost on our great-grandparents. In 1915, an article in the *Sarasota Times* educated readers about the virtues of sugar, which was said to provide one-half the nourishment that man needs. "Growing children need sweet foods and candy to help build up their muscular strength."

As to exercise, there were alternatives to the strenuous varieties. Why sweat when the San Juan Billiard Hall on Sixth Street offered snooker, a gentleman's game, as "a means of keeping fit without giving up too much precious time"? The ad asked, "Feeling sluggish, tired and a bit run down?" and explained, "You need exercise. A short time each day spent in our billiard room will lend zest to your every action and stimulate you mentally and physically. These fascinating games are the ounce of prevention that keeps the doctor away." The heck with apples.

For those who could not get in enough time at the pool hall and ended up in the hospital, the Navajo Sanitarium on Main Street offered radio treatment, violet rays and medicated baths and claimed to be the only sanitarium in the world that treated tuberculosis on the "No Cure, No Pay" plan.

It all seems a far city from today's complicated treatments and healthcare plans. But that's progress. And besides, Americans of the twenty-first century are too well educated and sophisticated to be duped into mail-order potions or miracle cures. Right.

Sarasota Memorial Hospital

NOVEMBER 2, 1925, WAS A MOMENTOUS DAY for Sarasota. Its new hospital was finally completed, and at three o'clock, hundreds of visitors embarked on a tour of the two-story, thirty-two-bed facility. Pronounced by the Sarasota *Herald* as "the greatest philanthropic undertaking which this county has ever known," the hospital was a proud structure, resplendent with Greek columns. Each visitor was greeted by Mrs. George B. Prime and Mrs. E.A. Smith, who had good reason to beam that beautiful Monday afternoon. As guests were led through, they were introduced to Gertrude, the hospital's doll mascot, dressed in a handmade party frock and donated to the hospital, the newspaper explained, to "help children regain their strength much more rapidly."

The effort to build the hospital was a by-product of Sarasota's real estate boom. For concurrent with the ritzy hotels, luxurious housing developments and glitzy advertisements wooing snowbirds were the community's efforts to use some of its new prosperity to assist the less fortunate. Usually it was the wives of the men who were the county's builders and boosters who gathered together at luncheons, teas, fashion shows, recitals and bridge parties to discuss how they could assist the poor and advance the quality of life in the blossoming community.

In October 1924, these ladies organized the Sarasota County Welfare Association to carry out the charitable work of the county and elected Mrs. George B. Prime president. Then they set upon the task of building Sarasota a hospital.

At the time, the town's only medical facility was the Halton Hospital on Pineapple Avenue, a private enterprise too small to keep pace with the burgeoning county in spite of the best efforts of its owner, Dr. Joseph Halton. (In the 1950s Halton was named Sarasota's Man of the Year for performing more than sixteen hundred operations on needy children.)

The association's first accomplishment was to purchase a tent in which to care for a tubercular patient. It purchased another tent shortly thereafter, but these were stopgap measures, the prelude to the construction of a bona fide hospital.

Plans were submitted by the prolific Thomas Reed Martin Studios, and a cost of $40,000.00 for construction and equipment was set. Mrs. E.A. Smith, whose husband would be elected mayor of Sarasota five times, led the fund-raising efforts. Mrs. Smith started with a building fund of only $2,197.87 and began a countywide campaign for contributions.

The thirty-two-bed Sarasota Hospital, November 2, 1925. *Sarasota County History Center*

All local businesses were beseeched for 100 percent employee participation, which would earn them recognition in the Sarasota *Herald*, itself a 100 percent participant, and a placard for the company window to inform passersby, "This company and its employees are 100 percent subscribers to the Sarasota Hospital Building Fund."

As is true in Sarasota today, individual benefactors were responsible for the largest contributions. Real estate man A S. Skinner underwrote an operating room, requesting that "it be second to none." Honoré and Potter Palmer Jr. gave five thousand dollars for an X-ray outfit in memory of their mother, Bertha Palmer. Others responded to the call for furnishing individual rooms at two hundred dollars apiece.

The finished product may have been quaint by today's standards. There was no air-conditioning, of course, so windows were left open even during operations. Patients came when they were sick (no formal admissions procedures) and stayed as long as the doctor, rather than the insurance company, felt necessary. (Maybe they really were the good old days.) It was the pride of Sarasota, run for a time by the ladies of the welfare association with a staff of fifteen plus fourteen doctors with staff privileges.

In 1926, a bond issue of $175,000 provided enough money to add an annex, and the hospital became known as Sarasota Municipal, with control turned over to the city.

THIS COMPANY
And Its Employees Are
100 per cent
Subscribers To The
Sarasota Hospital
Building Fund

Building fund poster used to raise money for the Sarasota Hospital. *Sarasota County History Center*

Today as Sarasota Memorial, the hospital has undergone numerous changes as it has expanded to keep pace with the ever growing county. A quote from its opening is still true today. "The new structure is a model of modern medical institutions," the newspaper pronounced, adding that Sarasota's citizens were glorifying "in the results of their good works."

Ringling's Ritz-Carlton Dream

JOHN RINGLING WAS A VISIONARY with multiple interests. He was a deal maker with the financial wherewithal, business acumen and connections to make things happen. He was a driving force behind Sarasota's growth, and his dreams for our city were usually prophetic; even those interrupted by the real estate crash of the 1920s and the Great Depression eventually came to fruition.

But one of his projects remained an empty shell on the sands of Longboat Key for nearly forty years, a monumental reminder that even the most famous tycoons have some failures.

Ringling wanted a hotel that would be the last word in luxury and a winter haven for the rich and famous of the Roaring Twenties. When he kicked off the drive to raise the funds to build it, the Sarasota *Herald* reported that it would cost $3 million to finish and would be "absolutely the finest and greatest tourist hotel...having every luxury and convenience." The Ritz-Carlton organization required $800,000 in good faith money. Ringling reportedly put in $400,000 of his own and the rest was to come from local investors. When $227,000 of that was pledged, building began.

Situated on sixty acres, the hotel was to be surrounded by three golf courses, one of which was actually completed. Each of its luxuriously appointed rooms would have a waterfront view. Constructed of brick nearly two feet thick in some places, the structure rose five stories and was accentuated by a large octagonal cupola with a winding staircase. There were magnificent courtyards, indoor fountains and columned archways galore.

But while the plan was grandiose, the timing was wrong. By 1926, the boom that had given birth to such fabulous projects was nearly over, and by the end of that year, the change in Sarasota's fortune was obvious. Although the Ritz-Carlton was only a few months from completion, Ringling had to call a halt to construction. In the early 1930s, Ringling purchased Owen Burns's El Vernona Hotel from the Prudential Company and changed its name to the John Ringling Hotel. But he continued to promise that work would soon begin again on the Ritz-Carlton. It never did; when he died in 1937, the hotel was still unfinished.

John Ringling North, his nephew and coexecutor of his estate, rekindled hopes in 1938. An article in the Sarasota *Herald-Tribune* was headlined "Ritz-Carlton, Circus King's Dream, Will Be Fulfilled This Year."

Within a few months of the completion of John Ringling's Ritz-Carlton Hotel, the money dried up and construction stopped. *Sarasota County History Center*

Nothing happened. The hotel next stirred interest when President Harry S Truman, on a visit in 1945, said the building would be suitable for a veterans hospital and indicated that he would recommend it be taken over by the government. But this, too, came to naught.

Ringling's extensive real estate holdings were purchased by the Arvida Corporation at the end of the 1950s, and while Arvida would complete Ringling's desire to develop Longboat Key, the old hotel, overgrown with tropical scrub and overrun with raccoons and wildlife, was left untouched. For locals, the unsecured structure was an inviting place to explore, picnic and rendezvous. At night, it was both alluring and forbidding; several people fell to their deaths there over the years. For tourists, the ghost hotel was the subject of questions and speculation.

Finally, in December 1964, demolition began, and by the beginning of 1965, the last trace of John Ringling's failed dream was hauled away. A few years later, however, the Arvida Corporation erected a luxury hotel close to the Ritz-Carlton site. Known as the Resort on Longboat Key, it fulfills Ringling's vision, welcoming affluent guests from all over to one of the most magnificent places in Florida.

The *Jomar*

John Ringling had a wealth of enterprises and they brought in millions of dollars. He lived in a grand manner: a Fifth Avenue apartment; a home in Alpine, New Jersey; a palatial showplace, Ca' d'Zan, in Sarasota; a world-class collection of art that he displayed in one of the loveliest museums in the country, his own. Ringling hobnobbed with the rich and famous and entertained them regally on his yacht, *Zalophus*. He was chauffeured in a Rolls-Royce, wore the finest cloths, smoked expensive cigars and sipped aged whiskey. But perhaps the most telling of his accoutrements was the *Jomar*.

Even in the flashy era of the Roaring Twenties, a personal railway car was something special, and Ringling's *Jomar* (a combination of John and Mable Ringling's first names), which was built in 1917, was one of the largest, measuring in at eighty-two feet and eleven inches. (Ringling's brother Charles's private car, the *Caledonia*, purchased in 1923, was said to measure eighty-five feet long.) In today's world of transport, only a richly appointed private Boeing 727 jet or an oceangoing yacht could compare.

Personal railway cars came into vogue as the rich man's status symbol during the Gilded Age, when ostentatious displays of wealth knew no bounds. Manufactured by the George Mortimer Pullman Company of Pullman, Illinois, each car was as unique as the customer's lavish taste. In Ringling's case, that included inlaid mahogany with intricately designed patterns, lamps with Tiffany shades, brass beds and a dining area with fine china, crystal and silverware.

The door on the rear platform opened into the observation room, which was furnished with eight comfortable wicker chairs, ceiling fans, bookcases, cabinets and an extension sofa. The next room, a guest bedroom, had a brass bed and upper berth. Mable's stateroom was next in line and was separated from John's larger stateroom by a bathroom with tub, shower, toilet and metal cigar holder—Mister John enjoyed a good smoke when he soaked. His room contained a large brass bed, sofa, mirrored dresser and space for his steamer trunk. The car weighed 175,400 pounds.

In the lavish dining room, six heavily upholstered chairs surrounded the table, and a handsome sofa opened to form an upper and lower berth. The last section of the car housed the servants quarters and the kitchen, where a chef prepared Ringling his delicious feasts.

Whenever the *Jomar* brought John and Mable to town, the *Sarasota Times* and the Sarasota *Herald* informed their readers. The car was parked on a rail spur that jutted into Sarasota Bay from Strawberry Avenue, not too far from City Pier, where the Ringling yacht *Zalophus* sometimes docked.

When John Ringling died in December 1936 (Mable had passed away in 1929), the *Jomar* was taken over by his nephew and executor of his estate, John Ringling North. North's tastes differed from those of his uncle, and by the end of the '30s, the car's original furnishing belonged to a different era. North remodeled the entire car, replacing the Victorian look with modern furnishings; he also lowered the ceiling to accommodate air-conditioning.

North used the *Jomar* extensively. He was an Olympic-class partier, and after holding court at the M'Toto Room lounge in the John Ringling Hotel until the wee hours, he'd often move the festivities to the *Jomar*, where they would continue until the sun came up. The car also served as his office, and from it, he ran the circus.

Over the years, the Ringlings and North entertained many luminaries aboard the *Jomar*, including General Pershing, leader of the American Expeditionary Forces in World War I; inventor Thomas Edison; President Warren G. Harding and movie director Cecil B. DeMille, who came to Sarasota to film *The Greatest Show on Earth*.

After the circus left Sarasota, the *Jomar* was moved to Venice, the new Circus City, then to Tampa, and finally it ended up in Louisiana, where it was badly vandalized. In 1989, the Friends of the Jomar Society was formed to rescue it. The group brought the dilapidated car back to Sarasota but was not able to restore it.

According to an article in the Sarasota *Herald-Tribune* by reporter Dale White, big plans are currently afoot for the *Jomar*. Harvey Vengroff of Vengroff Williams and Associates, a financial services firm, and restaurateur Bob Horne are planning to restore the grand old car to its former opulence with the help of volunteers. A multimillion-dollar entertainment complex is being planned on a former lumberyard off Fruitville Road. It is hoped that the *Jomar* will be one of its centerpieces.

The Sarasota Chamber of Commerce

During the Roaring Twenties, when newcomers were pouring into the Sunshine State by the tens of thousands, one reporter commented, "There is hardly a community in Florida large enough to have a post office that has not also a chamber of commerce engaged in the effort to tell the world of the superior advantage of that particular community." Drawing people to what was then considered America's last frontier was job one for developers, promoters, government officials and especially chambers of commerce, known for their efforts as "boosters."

Until then, Florida's charms had been sampled mainly by wealthy tourists drawn south by Henry Plant and Henry Flagler's railways and luxurious hotels. The Model T changed that, as did "Coolidge prosperity" and a zealous ad campaign designed by the state chamber of commerce that was 50 percent fact, 50 percent fiction and 100 percent colorful.

The chamber's campaign painted Florida as "A land of romance, legend, song and story, an emerald kingdom by southern seas, fanned by zephyrs laden with ozone from stately pines, watered by Lethe's copious libation." Wow!

With the state supplying such prose to lure the masses, it was then up to each local chamber to funnel as many as possible to its community.

Sarasota's chamber was up to the task. Its ongoing work helped transform Sarasota into the thriving city we enjoy today.

Like many of the state's chambers, Sarasota's began as a board of trade, established on November 11, 1911, with developer Owen Burns as its president. The editor of the *Sarasota Times*, C.V.S. Wilson, had noted that while hotels on the Manatee River were filled, Sarasota's were empty. "The reason is simple," he wrote. "We do not advertise." With thirty-seven members and a contribution from the Palmer Company, the new board of trade issued a brochure for nationwide distribution.

On November 24, 1920, the chamber of commerce was officially formed and began a campaign to draw tourists and new residents. A 1925 brochure called "Sarasota: A City of Glorified Opportunity" told readers that "God lingered over the effect to be produced in Sarasota County, and for all these years Nature seems to have rested in rapt contemplation of her rich and varied charms." Good stuff. The chamber also sponsored Post Card Week, a statewide competition to see which community could mail out the most postcards to northern friends and relatives.

Radio station WJBB, "the Voice of the Semi-Tropics," sponsored by the chamber, provided listeners around the country with music, broadcasts from the winter headquarters of the Ringling Brothers circus and colorful commentaries about Sarasota. One listener wrote from Oregon, "Sarasota seems to be a live city and will derive great benefit from your programs."

As the freewheeling 1920s made way for the somber Depression of the '30s, the chamber maintained its effort, supporting Works Progress Administration projects and urging construction of the Lido Casino as a way of increasing summer tourism.

In the 1950s, the chamber formed the Committee of 100 to attract business and light industry. It also began a quest to draw summer tourists; part of its campaign involved collaborating with the state chamber to stomp out the ugly rumor in the northern press that Florida was hot during the summer. We were, after all, the Air-Conditioned City.

Today, the organization is a key player in every aspect of Sarasota's growth. As Karl H. Grismer noted in *The Story of Sarasota*, "To relate the activities of the Chamber of Commerce since 1920 would be like repeating the history of the city."

Wildcat!

FINANCIAL FREEWHEELING WAS AS SYNONYMOUS with the 1920s as hooch, flappers and Tin Lizzies. The roads to Easy Street were many, including stocks and bonds (on margin, of course), real estate speculation and, if you were fortunate enough to live in Texas, Oklahoma, or Sarasota, oil drilling. Oil? In Sarasota? Yes, indeed. For a brief and glorious moment, a covey of Sarasotans was convinced that a sea of black gold lay just beneath our sandy soil.

The Sarasota *Herald* was the first to announce that there could be more to real estate than a plot for your dream home. A banner headline on January 1, 1926, blared: "CHAS. COULTER COMING TO VIEW OIL SITUATION." The story explained that this nationally known geologist would soon arrive with a team of experts to determine the probabilities "for a big strike in the territory." Although Coulter stressed that he was not here to arouse false hope, the paper assured readers that there was "every indication that in his announcements will be found plenty of encouragement for the people of this district." Coulter's word, it was said, was accepted by oil men the world over. Kenneth Hauer, head of the Biscayne Oil Company, was in charge of drilling, and he was "optimistic but very conservative." In fact, said the *Herald*, "[Hauer] has frankly stated that it is his belief that oil is to be found and in large quantities, but he wishes to give no positive statement nor arouse any undue hopes until oil is actually flowing from a well in this district."

Sarasota was immediately fired with excitement. The El Vernona Hotel (demolished in 1998 as the John Ringling Towers) had formally opened the night before, and the entire front page of the paper was filled with accounts of the festivities. That oil would soon be discovered seemed to make the picture perfect.

It wasn't until the end of 1926, when it was becoming apparent that the real estate rush was just about played out, that the next chapter in the oil story was splashed across the front page of the *Herald*: "ACTUAL DRILLING FOR OIL IS NOW ASSURED." Hauer had met with the leading businessmen of the community and discovered "sufficient encouragement in the geological surveys and in the interests shown by the Capitalists of this section" to begin drilling. He was said to express in a most conservative manner that there were great possibilities in this section. Drilling equipment was brought in and set up on the site deemed most likely to gush. It was

The Associated Oil and Gas derrick, erected in 1927 near Englewood on John Ringling's property. *Sarasota County History Center*

in Englewood and was soon called the Ringling tract. John Ringling, who owned oil wells in other sections of the country, was playing it close to the chest. "I have nothing to say at this time with reference to oil possibilities in Sarasota. That is a matter of which I know as little as you. Mr. Hauer is the man to see, he is the oil man. Naturally, I hope that we find oil, and in great quantities here."

In spite of the professed caution, oil was being talked up throughout the county. In fact, it was the number one topic, and real estate offices, which were feeling the effects of the downturn, were gearing up to sell leases on oil fields.

By March 1927, the first well was ready to be spudded in, and conservative statements gave way to the bombastic prose that had characterized real estate sales and marketing. Executives of the Community Oil Corporation, selling stock in local oil, "expressed the belief that within the next several months, Sarasota would buzz with activity caused by the discovery here of an oil field equal to those in the Mid-Continent section."

The Ringling tract was twelve miles east of Englewood, and the roads to it were crowded with onlookers, who were offered free cigars and refreshments and the chance to shake hands with baseball great Rogers Hornsby of the New York Giants. Hauer promised the excited crowd, "Should oil be found, and we are

SARASOTA HERALD

Today's Weather

SARASOTA, FLORIDA, SUNDAY, MARCH 13, 1927

FIRST OIL WELL TO BE STARTED HERE TODAY

Condemned Men Escape Prison And Terrorize Illinois

Faced By Death They Break For Liberty Again

Second Attempt Made by These Men, First Having Been Frustrated Several Weeks Ago, Five Men Shot in Efforts to Escape; Guards "Covered" With Guns by Trusties, Impressed Deputy Sheriff Into Service as Their Chauffeur on Mad Break

MERLE EVANS' BAND IN FINA L CONCERT OF SEASON TODAY

Rogers Hornsby Will Officially Start The Work

Free Cigars and Refreshments For all Who Attend "Spudding In" of First Well on Ringling Tract This Afternoon; All Roads Expected to be Crowded With Visitors Bound For Site of Well; Kenneth Hauer to Give Signal For Starting

DEATH PENALTY IS URGED FOR THEFT CRIME

States Attorneys Would have Death Penalty For Robbery Where Gun is Used

LIDO BEACH AGAIN THE SCENE OF FROLIC AND FUN WITH THE DUTTONS

HORSE RACING DEALT DEATH BLOW BY MARTIN

Pompano Track Closes Doors After Officers Are Arrested; Governor's Order

BLIZZARD IN WEST CREATES GREAT HAVOC

One Death, Disrupted Train Service, Blocked Highways and Marooned Motor Cars

DAWES IS NOT YET CANDIDATE FOR PRESIDENT

Declares If He is Running for President He Does Not Yet Know It

BRITISH FORCES QUELL TROUBLE IN SHANGHAI

Large Body of Armed Troops Try to Enter International Settlement; Are Repulsed

COMMUNITY OIL COMPANY FINDS INTEREST SHOWN HERE DAILY INCREASES

SENATOR KING NOT PERMITTED TO VISIT HAITI

Haitian Government Resenting Attacks of Senator Close Door to His Visit

MAN ARRESTED AS DRIVER OF TRUCK WHICH KILLED MAN

SUITOR SLASHES WOMAN WHO WILL NOT MARRY HIM

BURGLARS ENTERED CLUB HOUSE AT THE BOBBY JONES COURSE

DINNER GIVEN BY L. D. REAGIN FOR J. J. McGRAW AT VENICE HUGE SUCCESS

Czechs To Play At Oil Spudding Ceremony Today

Missourians In Sarasota Urged To Attend Game

ATLANTIC COAST LINE ANNOUNCES ITS EXPENDITURES

That Sarasota might be atop a sea of black gold was headline news. *Sarasota County History Center*

certain that it will, the first so-called 'boom' will be a gentle zephyr compared to a cyclone." The *Herald* proclaimed that the event would mark a new and mighty era for the state.

Also reminiscent of the land boom were the full-page advertisements. One showed a picture of a gusher and told perspective investors, "Florida 100 Percent Oil Possibility," and "You May Take Out a Bankroll."

There were three ways to make out in oil, and everyone could afford to play. For as little as $10.00, you could purchase two-hundredths of an interest in four leases. For $12.50 to $20.00 per acre, you could lease tracts of five to eighty acres. Fifty dollars would buy one-fortieth interests in four leases—four chances to win! And if you didn't want to make your way to the Mira Mar Hotel to sign up, a handy coupon was attached for your convenience.

But alas, not a drop of oil ever trickled, much less gushed, from the imposing derrick. What was struck was sulfur water. It jetted out in great abundance and stunk worse than the cigars handed out by Hornsby.

The Champion of Champions

NOWHERE WAS THE SPIRIT OF the Roaring Twenties more alive than in the world of sports. In baseball, "the Sultan of Swat," Babe Ruth, was pounding 'em out of ballparks; on the gridiron, "the Galloping Ghost," Red Grange, was running wild; in the ring, "the Manassa Mauler," Jack Dempsey, with fists like granite and a jaw to match, was felling opponents with knockout blows. Their exploits generated front-page news for a sports-mad public, and many of their record-breaking feats were to stand unchallenged for decades.

One of the greatest of these sports legends was a young man who performed his feats in a white, long-sleeved shirt and tie and knickers. Polite, self-effacing and mannerly, he was a Southern gentleman in every sense of the word and every parent's idea of what a son should be—except when he lost his temper. Robert Tyre Jones Jr., aka Bobby Jones, was an amateur who never turned pro and who set the golfing world on its ear.

He was twenty-four years old in 1926, when he came to Sarasota to open the municipal golf course, soon to be known as the Bobby Jones course. Behind him was a string of victories, including the U.S. Open, 1923 and 1926; the U.S. Amateur, 1924 and 1925 and the British Open, 1926. Ahead were two more U.S. Opens and one more British Amateur. Of the six tournaments he played in 1930, he won five, one of them by thirteen strokes. In terms of popularity, only today's Tiger Woods compares.

In 1926, Jones and Sarasota, both riding a crest of popularity, were a natural match. The community took pride in claiming to be the birthplace of golf America (we weren't), since J. Hamilton Gillespie of Scotland laid out the first links here in 1886. And the importance of golf to our future had already been recognized by the *Sarasota Times*, which declared, "a golf-less tourist resort in Florida is in much the same class as a production of '*Hamlet*' with the star character left out."

For the official dedication, the course was festively decorated. Bobby cut the ribbon and drove the first ball straight and true. It was a windy day, but Jones managed a 38 out and a 35 in. The *Herald* reported that he "played his prettiest golf on the short thirteen. He was on in one and with his putter, Calamity Jane, sank a 20-foot putt for a birdie two." Jones was presented with a Pierce-Arrow, one of the finest cars of the era, by the pleased citizens of Sarasota, and he promised a return match.

Sarasota's master of ceremonies, Jules Brazil, presents Bobby Jones, the king of golf, a 1926 Pierce-Arrow. *Sarasota County History Center*

When he came back in 1927, he was again front-page news, with the paper asserting he was "royally welcomed and splendidly entertained while here." Reporters from the *Chicago Tribune* and the *New York Times* motion picture newsweekly were among those on hand to follow the match and photograph Bobby at a gala dinner at the Mira Mar Hotel. The chamber of commerce promised to entertain Jones and his golfing partner, Watts Gunn, in "such regal manner befitting their stature in the golfing world." There would be "no tiresome speeches, no moments of dullness."

Not too long after the festive evening, Sarasota's real estate market collapsed. But Bobby Jones's star continued to shine. Having "no more worlds to conquer," he retired from competition in 1930, the year he won the Grand Slam, and was treated to his second ticker-tape parade down Broadway in New York City. By then he was an Atlanta attorney and planned to make films teaching how to play golf. The *New York Times* editorialized that Jones "with dignity, quits the memorable scene upon which he nothing common did nor mean."

In 1948, Jones was struck with syringomyelia, a disease that destroys sensory and motor nerves. He was in constant pain for the remainder of his life, yet his spirit remained undaunted. Of his disease he once said, "Remember, we play the ball as it lies."

Jones died in 1971; among the many tributes to him was this: "He never lost any of the values that make up the complete man: humanity, humor, consideration and courtesy to all about him."

The next time you're on the thirteenth hole at the Bobby Jones course, crouched over to sink your putt, remember that you're standing near the same spot where one of the greatest men in the sport used Calamity Jane to take a birdie. Don't be nervous.

The Chicago Connection

Sarasota had an abundance of the right stuff necessary to become a successful community: inviting white sand beaches; the alluring, jewel-like sparkle of the Gulf of Mexico and Sarasota Bay; the lush, brightly colored foliage; picturesque multicolored sunsets and a salubrious climate all added up to an unmatched tropical paradise. But it took more than a scenic setting to become today's desirable destination. What helped to make Sarasota happen was an astute group of investors, developers and boosters with the vision and the wherewithal to woo wealthy newcomers. For this, Sarasota could thank its Chicago connection.

It was the Windy City that supplied many of the people who forged this Gulf Coast paradise into a snowbird's winter retreat, a vacation spot that evolved into the fast-paced year-round city we enjoy so much today.

The Chicago migration to Sarasota started in the winter of 1910. We were little more than a cow town with fewer than a thousand souls, two of whom, A.B. Edwards and J.H. Lord, placed a small advertisement in a Chicago newspaper touting the charms of this unknown section of Florida, America's last frontier. Bertha Honoré Palmer, a world-famous society woman, read it and was convinced to come down for a look-see. Her arrival was a momentous occasion for Sarasota. A.B. Edwards referred to it as the most important event in Sarasota's history. She and her entourage were escorted around and marveled at the pristine loveliness of the area. Captivated by Sarasota Bay, she invested heavily here and built Spanish Oaks for her winter retreat in Osprey. For the first time Sarasota, an unknown one-horse town in a wilderness state, was front-page news in the national and international press, which closely followed Palmer's activities.

Her pronouncements about Sarasota's beauty piqued the interest of Owen Burns, another Chicago resident.

Burns, an avid fisherman, came a few months later. In those days, the local waters were a cornucopia of all manner of fish and offered unparalleled sport fishing. But it was Burns who was hooked and stayed. He bought out the holdings of the Florida Mortgage and Investment Company from John Hamilton Gillespie, and began a development campaign that continued from 1910 through 1926, producing some of Sarasota's finest housing developments and buildings. An account of his early activities was described in the *Sarasota Times* thus: "He purchased a tract of earth

Bertha Palmer, the Chicago socialite and woman of the world whose visit to Sarasota in 1910 showed the spotlight on us for the first time. *Sarasota County History Center*

which natives considered of little value, filled it, graded and ornamented it, cut it up into lots…and had given Sarasota the greatest boost in the history of that pretty place." By the time of the real estate crash, Burns had built the apartments and stores at Herald Square, the quaint bungalows of Burns Court, the Washington Park subdivision, the El Vernona Apartments and Sarasota's hallmark hotel, the El Vernona Hotel. Burns's construction company built John and Mable Ringling's mansion, Ca' d'Zan, remodeled the Sarasota Yacht Club into the Sunset Apartments and, working in conjunction with John Ringling, dredged and beautified Longboat Key, Lido Key, Bird Key and St. Armand's Key. He also built the original John Ringling Causeway. In terms of Sarasota "town building," no developer has ever accomplished more or left a more lasting imprint.

Mrs. Palmer was instrumental in bringing architect Thomas Reed Martin from Chicago to Sarasota to design her retreat, Spanish Oaks. Martin, too, stayed on, and his prolific output of homes and buildings is still everywhere to be seen—the Municipal Auditorium, the Chidsey Library (today's Sarasota County History Center) as well as approximately five hundred homes sprinkled throughout Sarasota. His son, Frank Martin, designed the magnificent Hazzard fountain, which was recently renovated and graces the front of the auditorium.

Also coming to Sarasota from Chicago was Andrew McAnsh, who journeyed down and made the city council an offer it didn't refuse. He would build a world-class apartment building, hotel and auditorium in downtown to attract wealthy vacationers if the city would grant him a few piddling concessions: no taxes for ten years and free light and water. It would, and he did. The result was one of

Sarasota's finest complexes, the Mira Mar Apartments, Hotel and Auditorium on Palm Avenue. The Mediterranean Revival motif that characterized these buildings became the signature for Sarasota designs. He extended his development onto Siesta Key, where his Mira Mar Casino was a hotspot for beachgoers and diners and dancers. Two giant flood lamps lit up the gulf for nighttime bathing. The real casino action, however, was back at his auditorium, where another Chicago concern, Conrad and Locke, operated a gaming room offering roulette, dice and card games.

When the real estate boom was in full swing, Sarasota was connected to Chicago by the Atlantic Coast Line train, and newcomers arrived in town aboard the Dixie Flyer, Dixie Limited, Seminole or Flamingo, lured south by colorfully worded, bombastic prose to vacation or seek their fortune in the skyrocketing real estate market. In 1925, one of the busiest corners in the world was said to be the intersection of Chicago's Michigan Avenue and Twelfth Street, a bustling shopping and theatre district. Thousands walked past each day and saw a giant billboard advertising Sarasota's charms. Radio listeners could tune in Sarasota's own station WJBB, "the Voice of the Semi-Tropics," which was sponsored by the chamber of commerce and broadcast the virtues of life in Sarasota around the nation.

Some were drawn here by Roger Flory, a Chicago lawyer who gave up his profession to begin a lucrative and long-lasting career in Sarasota real estate. He published the Sarasota Visitors' Guide annually from the 1920s through the 1960s for general distribution and wrote of his new home, "Sarasota has a personality that sets it apart from every other place in the world…and once you are exposed to it you want to stay forever. If you must leave, it will not be for long." His comprehensive guides grew with the community and showcased everything there was to do and see in Sarasota. Flory, a key civic leader, was also instrumental in getting the storied Lido Casino built in order to increase summer tourism.

At the beginning of 1927 the Sarasota *Herald* headlined the news that another important Chicago native, Stanley Field, "noted financier," planned to build a $350,000 mansion on Little Sarasota Bay, north of the Palmer estates. It was to be a palatial home, situated on several hundred acres. The *Herald* called it "one of the most impressive and attractive 'country' homes in America." Mr. and Mrs. Field were referred to as the "Who's Who in Blue Book Circles." Built by the firm of Stevenson and Cameron, who constructed the Sarasota County Courthouse, the showplace was offered in 1957 to "any Club which would use it for Club purposes." Asking price? A paltry $175,000. In June of that year the Field Club was formed.

It's impossible to say what Sarasota would have become without its deep-rooted connection to Chicago. But without the likes of Palmer, Burns, McAnsh, Martin, Flory, Field and others, it certainly would have been less. Much less.

The City of Glorified Opportunity

IN THE DAYS WHEN ADVERTISING the virtues of Florida often went hand in hand with exaggeration, the Sarasota *Herald* admonished local boosters, "The Truth About Sarasota Is Good Enough." No need to be deceptive about one of the most beautiful communities in the country. Tell the truth, and they will come.

On October 3, 1926, its first anniversary, the newspaper followed its own advice and printed a special edition that sang the praises of our rapidly growing town. The editors invited the public to send copies of the paper, rolled and mailed for just ten cents, to their northern neighbors to influence them to come to Sarasota for the winter. Nine sections showcased what was called "The City of Glorified Opportunity."

Thus was launched what would become known as the Mail-Away edition, a combination newspaper and chamber of commerce promotion that presented in print and pictures the numerous reasons Sarasota was a must-see destination.

The picture the paper painted was of an ever growing city, a desirable winter retreat with newly built hotels, banks, restaurants, bridges to the out-islands and spectacular housing developments. Readers were assured that one didn't need to be rich to enjoy the winter here. Why, the price of a round trip was a mere $100.00 to $200.00, an apartment could be had for $400.00 to $500.00 for the entire season, food would cost only $3.50 to $4.00 a day ($.59 was the price of the average meal in local cafeterias) and the main attractions, the fabulous beaches, were free. (To assuage any fears about the local yokels, an article reported that everybody, from citizens to the Sarasota police force, was taught to be polite.)

In 1953, the editors hit on a fresh idea for the Mail-Away. They would choose a vacationing family and follow them throughout their stay for a photo-essay on Sarasota's various attractions. When Robert Price signed in with the chamber of commerce's visitors bureau, he became the six thousandth visitor to arrive that year, and he and his wife, Joyce, and their three-year-old daughter, Robin, were rewarded with a whirlwind tour. A crew of photographers followed them to the attractions, and the resulting article was headlined "Typical Family Enjoys Hospitality of Sarasota."

Looking back at the photographs, it's clear the Sarasota of 1953 had more in common with the 1926 version than today's speeded-up city. The Prices basked on

Left: Summer visitors Mr. and Mrs. Price dance to the music of Rudy Bundy at the Lido Casino.

Below: The Price family at the entrance to the Sarasota Jungle Gardens.

Opposite Above: Posing in front of the sign for the winter headquarters of the Ringling Brothers and Barnum & Bailey Circus.

Opposite Below: The happy family leaves the Lido Casino. *Joyce Price*

RINGLING BROS
AND
BARNUM & BAILEY
COMBINED SHOWS
WINTER QUARTERS

the beach without a condo in sight, visited a downtown that was the center of retail and business for the entire community and enjoyed a lazy holiday atmosphere.

They dined at the Casa Marina Room at the Lido Casino and had their picture taken with quintessential bandmaster Rudy Bundy. Like many tourists, they went to the Glass Blower's shop on the North Trail, Ca' d'Zan, the John and Mable Ringling Museum of Art and the Sarasota Art Association. In case such cultural offerings wouldn't pull in enough visitors, they were also pictured at the Jungle Gardens, Horn's Cars of Yesterday, Texas Jim Mitchell's Reptile Farm and the winter headquarters of the Ringling Brothers and Barnum & Bailey Circus, one of the top attractions in the state. Still not interested in coming down? How about a picture of Dad fishing from the Ringling Causeway, boarding one of the fishing boats at City Pier, playing shuffleboard or just relaxing on the beach? The photographs underlined the copy's assertion that we were indeed "The Nation's Winter Playground, Where the Sun Shines Every Day."

Somehow omitted from the article, recalled Mrs. Price, were the red tide that had left parts of the beach heaped with dead fish, a hurricane that had recently brushed by and mosquitoes so thick that her family had to run from their hotel room to the water to avoid them.

But none of that kept the Prices from falling in love with this welcoming wonderland. Robert Price told the reporters, "Sarasota has everything…I'll be back again, and I hope to make my home here."

And come back they did. After visits almost every year, Robert and Joyce returned in 1972 to settle in a vastly different but still beautiful Sarasota. They never regretted the move, says Joyce, who still lives here. (Robert has since passed away.)

The Prices were one of many northern families attracted by the Mail-Aways. But boosterism was to go out of vogue with journalists, who now see their role as reporting on rather promising business and growth. By the newspaper's fiftieth anniversary, the special editions had been discontinued.

The Air-Conditioned City

EVEN THOUGH THE NORTHERN PRESS printed scurrilous stories that Sarasota's sunny clime was less than comfortable during the summertime, most Sarasotans knew that it didn't get that hot here—not all *that* hot.

Decades before mechanical air-conditioning existed, the locals referred to their hometown as the Air-Conditioned City, fanned by gentle gulf and bay breezes. For them the hottest day in August was preferable to any October, November, December, January, February and most of March above the Mason-Dixon Line.

In the mid-1950s, the weather battle really heated up. Our ever active chamber of commerce, seeking to entice more summer tourists, felt duty bound to debunk the slander that Florida actually got hot. An article in The *News* proclaimed, "Records prove that while temperatures soar over the Nation, it's comfortable here." The *News* advised readers to "Beat the Heat! Stay in Air-Conditioned Sarasota where it's C-O-O-L." It reported that while New Yorkers were suffering sunstrokes and Washington was blistering through ninety-eight-degree days, we were "enjoying a temperate 87 degrees."

In his 1955 Sarasota Visitors' Guide, Roger Flory laid out the facts: "Summer nights are particularly cool! The reason is that either the evening is cooled by refreshing afternoon thundershowers, or fresh sea breezes from the Gulf of Mexico descend over Sarasota with a cooling sensation that is so inviting to a good night of sleep in the summertime."

Then the Florida State Chamber of Commerce jumped into the fray, announcing that it was going to invest heavily in "breaking down the fallacy that it is hot here in the summer."

As Florida promoters trumpeted to battle, those who actually lived through the summers here availed themselves of time-tested ways to beat the, uh, warmth. Shirtsleeves were worn instead of suits, and during the slow-paced summer months, casually dressed businesspeople often took a long mid-afternoon break on the Ringling Bridge, casting for fish, drinking a cool one and enjoying the breeze.

Downtown, overhangs provided shade along the sidewalks, as did the giant memorial oaks that lined Main Street east from Orange Avenue. Ladies often carried parasols, and handheld fans were common. Businesses as well as homes

The Air-Conditioned City. *Sarasota County History Center*

left front and rear doors open for cross-ventilation, while ceiling fans stirred the breezes and table fans whizzed back and forth. Autos had butterfly windows that cranked open to funnel air directly onto driver and passenger.

In the 1930s, an announcement for a popularity contest and dance at the Mira Mar Auditorium noted that guests would be "cooled with electric fans and tons of natural ice." (Electric fans were called "a portable breeze.")

But the great equalizer was air-conditioning. At the beginning of 1940, Walgreen's Bay Drugs announced that along with modern fluorescent lighting, its building would be outfitted with a unit "especially designed for Florida's mild climate." Other businesses followed suit, but not as quickly as one might suppose. While Walgreen's had been designed with air-conditioning in mind, existing businesses and homes were not. As late as 1956, the developer of Bay Shore described the seven essentials of the perfect Florida house; these included a screened porch and sliding glass doors, but not air-conditioning.

For most buildings, the conversion began with window units. The J.H. Cobb company advertised that one could "stop sweltering and start relaxing" with its Frigidaire unit, which provided "Mountain Crisp comfort all summer long."

As more and more merchants brought in air, doors were shut to keep the coolness inside. Window stickers were posted to let passersby know that business was open—and C-O-O-L.

Our comfort zone soon became dependent on manufactured coolness. It was everywhere: shops, offices, cars, churches and finally even schools. The thought of not having it at home, too, became intolerable, especially after gulf and bay breezes were blocked along the shoreline by high-rise condominiums.

Today, not having air-conditioning is akin to not having electricity. And while screened porches and sliding doors are still desirable in the Florida home, it is central air that has become essential. We really have become the air-conditioned city.

The Mosquito Wars

FOR THE NORTHERN SNOWBIRDS WHO flocked here in the 1950s, Sarasota was paradise, but with two perennial problems: the summer heat (the chamber of commerce pronouncements notwithstanding) and those damn mosquitoes. Air-conditioning finally arrived in the '50s, but it would take more than air-conditioners to defeat those intolerable mosquitoes. It would take war! And it would not be over until red-blooded Sarasotans could venture from their homes at night, even during the summer, without hearing the warning whine of the dreaded *Aedes taeniohynchus*—the mosquito that traveled in black clouds at twilight, coating any tender-fleshed human unwary enough to venture outside.

It's been lost to the ages who fired the first slap, and whether it was a hit (more likely a miss), but skirmishes began with the arrival of the first settler. Nellie Lawrie, one of the original Scottish colonists, wrote in her journal, "A Cracker came along one day and told Mother, 'What them ants don't eat, the sandflies do, and what they leave behind, the mosquitoes git.'" For the pioneers, protection consisted of mosquito netting, staying inside and swatting—lots of swatting. Another early settler wrote that his dog was bitten to death

By the 1920s more sophisticated offensive measures were employed to hit them where it hurt: in their pupae. According to J.B. Privett, who owned Privett's Drugstore, the city collected crank case oil from filling stations. A quantity of the oily fluid was poured into open sewers, causing a film that kept mosquito larvae from hatching. Privett also said that filling a sock full of sawdust soaked in grease and sinking it in a flooded area would keep mosquitoes out of an area for almost the entire summer. June 21, 1926 was the beginning of Cleanup Week in Sarasota, a campaign by every householder to join together to rid the entire district of mosquitoes. Dr. John R. Scully, the city and county health commissioner, used the slogan "Death to the Mosquito" as a rallying cry to get rid of them, "whatever their size, color or breed." They missed a few, however.

The first uniformed soldiers enlisted in the mosquito war were local Boy Scouts, who patrolled the city, collecting cans and rubbish that might otherwise fill with water and offer larvae a place to hatch. Ushers (they wore uniforms, too) sprayed at the feet of moviegoers at the Edwards Theatre to keep the swatting to a minimum during show time.

Left: Mel Williams (left) and Bud Davis—members of the Dawn Patrol—stand by one of the biplanes used by Sarasota County to eradicate mosquitoes.
Sarasota County History Center

Below: County mosquito foggers—just something for the neighborhood kids to run behind.
Sarasota County History Center

The war was obviously being won by the mosquitoes. Each season, black clouds of humming skeeters swarmed through Sarasota like Sherman through Georgia. Natives who had never known the possibility of pleasant outdoor life during summer evenings tolerated the situation, but the chamber of commerce knew it was preventing summer tourism and long-term growth.

Enter J. Melton Williams. He would be to Sarasota's mosquitoes what Patton was to the Nazis. Appointed director of mosquito control in December 1945, he waged an unrelenting campaign. It could be argued that as much as any individual, he turned Sarasota into a year-round resort.

Williams fought the mosquitoes on land, in the air and on the beaches, with planes and jeeps spewing clouds of death and destruction with DDT. His arsenal contained four specially equipped planes; locals called the flights Operation Mosquito and the Dawn Patrol. There were setbacks on the way to victory. A headline in the late 1940s in the Sarasota *Herald-Tribune* reported, "Mosquitos win over DDT. Planes Grounded." In June of 1948, the *Herald* warned, "Mansonia mosquito defies ordinary measures."

Williams counterattacked, increasing the strength of the DDT. Chlordane and later malathion were added to the arsenal, routinely bathing not only mosquitoes but the children who would appear at the first sound of the fogger and run behind the clouds of spray.

Insectisides were part of everyday life. Every excursion to the drive-in required Pic, a coil of insecticide that would be lit with a match and burn throughout the movie, as necessary to a good time there as the backseat.

Williams urged every citizen to become a soldier, serving the war effort by keeping lawns mowed, picking up empty containers and spraying around the house. The people of Sarasota responded enthusiastically; they knew whom to thank for their newfound evening freedom. Letters of thanks to Williams frequently appeared in the newspaper. This one from Douglas Graham in the 1950s was typical: "Mr. Williams has done a remarkably fine job for this city; we should give him high praise for his work."

A Black-and-White Sarasota

It's easy to look back on Sarasota's yesteryears with fond nostalgia for simpler, happier times. But those idyllic days we recall so wistfully never existed for many Sarasotans, our black citizens. For all Sarasota's attractions in those bygone years, it was still a small town in the South, and to the blacks who lived here, the good old days were often not very good at all.

The Roaring Twenties were particularly difficult. The era that was notable for the real estate boom that transformed Sarasota from a dusty fishing village into a destination for the rich and famous also saw the national resurgence of the Ku Klux Klan.

There were no lynches in Sarasota, although accounts of them and floggings in other parts of the South were regularly on page 1 of the local paper. But Klan Number 72 of the Invisible Empire was alive and well here, and its activities were often reported in the *Sarasota Times* and the Sarasota *Herald*.

The papers also printed Klan advertisements: "NO HONEST RIGHT THINKING, WHITE American can CONSCIENTIOUSLY oppose the Knights." The Klan explained it stood "not to crush the downtrodden, but to PROTECT THE WEAK, ASSIST THE NEEDY and to succor the distressed." Klan parades were well attended. "KU KLUX KLAN OUT ON PARADE," ran one headline. "By 7:30, Five Points was a moving mass of people anxiously waiting for the parade of hidden faces to start."

In an effort to raise money to build a "Klavern [Klan headquarters] which will exceed anything of its kind south of Atlanta," Sarasota's Klan engaged the Morton Circus for a week's performance. Preceding the event were half-page ads announcing "KLAN CIRCUS" with its "Stupendous Aggregation of Celebrated Circus Arenic Stars." News stories kept readers informed of the circus's success: "KLAN CIRCUS IS HIT AGAIN WITH CAPACITY CROWD." Along with the "programs of select circus acts of highest class" were opportunities for local participation. The winner of the Miss Sarasota Popularity Contest was crowned on the center platform, followed the next evening by the marriage of a very popular young couple...under the dome of the big circus top.

The Klan's emergence paralleled the white establishment's harassment of blacks. Groups of black men were frequently arrested and then charged with idleness and vagrancy, gambling or liquor violations. Typical was a Sarasota *Herald* headline: "Doing

Segregated class at Booker Elementary School. *Dorothye Smith collection. Sarasota County History Center*

The music teacher visits the Laurel "colored" School, circa 1922. *Sherry Borza Collection, Cora Heywood, Red Cross nurse photo album. Sarasota County History Center*

The Woolworth lunch counter at the Ringling Shopping Center. On March 2, 1960, a group of eleven African Americans sat down here and were refused service. The group was described as orderly and their leader, Gene Carnegie, told the *News*, "We could have easily brought 40 people in here and another 200 outside picketing, but that would incite trouble and would not be in the best interests of the community." A *Tampa Tribune* editorial reprinted in the story called such demonstrations, "ill advised." *A. Richard Baron*

The beaming Miss Newtown 1961, Angela Maulsby, and her escort, Marvin Gaines, pose for the camera. *Josie Gaines collection. Sarasota County History Center*

Nothing But It Costs. Sarasota Negroes Find They Are Not Lilies of the Field." The story recounted how twenty-nine black men were rounded up in a pool room, charged with "idleness" and fined twenty-five dollars each, plus costs. The arrests were undertaken because the sheriff had received numerous complaints that it was impossible to find labor. Employers complained that wages were so high that after a few days, most laborers quit and gambled their money away. Despite their reported high wages, the men in the pool room did not have enough money to pay their fines and ended up on road gangs, thereby conveniently easing the county's labor shortage. In another story, "Judge Hard on Negro Idlers," the paper reported that "every Negro seen loafing on the street was questioned." Another was titled "Four Negro Vagrants Will Work for County 60 Days."

At its peak, the Klan had five million members, but by 1930 it had lost much of its power. Still, the vicissitudes of segregation and the concept of separate but equal facilities, which, while always separate were never equal, hung on.

Blacks Sarasotans were forced to the back of buses, drank from specially designated water fountains, were presented with restrooms labeled "Men," "Women" and "Colored" and were prohibited from entering most restaurants, theatres and schools. When the new bus terminal was opened on Main Street and Orange Avenue in 1943, it was noted that it was "equipped with a lunch room for Negro patrons."

In the 1950s, battle was finally joined between Sarasota blacks and whites. The issue: the use of city and county beaches, which had always been closed to blacks.

The civil rights movement and Supreme Court decisions encouraged the blacks, but the county threatened to sell its beaches rather than integrate them, and the city gave police the authority to close all beaches to "prevent racial strife." A county commissioner was reported to have told a crowd of blacks, "When you can buy a beach for forty thousand dollars, let me know."

The county appointed a group of citizens to study the issue and devise a solution to "the Negro beach problem." (In 1955, two proposed sites for all-black beaches had been rejected: one north of City Island and the other north of Bird Key, with access by a county-run ferry.) Pulitzer prize–winning author and longtime resident MacKinlay Kantor joined the fray by threatening to write an article for national publication titled "Sarasota Cheats Its Black Children" if a beach was not found for them. The *News* editorialized, "The time for the county commission to act is now, while the NAACP is weak in Sarasota County." After all, it said, "a good summer tourist season is just around the corner; let's not spoil it."

Eventually, a pool for black citizens was completed in the Newton area and over time, beaches, schools and other aspects of life in Sarasota were integrated. The days when a black man was expected to move off the sidewalk when passing a white are long past. But many black Sarasotans still remember the time most white Sarasotans would prefer to forget, when racial hatred and unfairness divided our little town.

The Memorial Oaks of Main Street

NOT TOO LONG AGO, A stroll along Main Street from Orange Avenue east to the Atlantic Coastline Railway Station was like a journey through a Norman Rockwell painting. There were homes with porches, nicely kept lawns and people to greet as you walked by. A buffering strip of grass divided the sidewalk from the street and in the evening, old-fashioned domed street lamps cast a comforting glow. But most pleasing of all were the majestic shade trees that lined the street.

They were our Memorial Oaks—181 of them, a tree for each Sarasotan who had marched off to fight in World War I. By the end of 1954, they had grown to full and lush maturity.

Therein lay the problem. Sarasota was starting its push to progress, and the trees...well, they were standing, however proudly, in the way. Ken Thompson, the city manager, told a reporter, "The presence of trees along Main Street has undoubtedly curtailed development of the city's main street as a business street." A city commissioner put it more bluntly: "It's either the oaks or progress." The city's leaders wanted progress.

A group of citizens disagreed and quickly formed the Friends of Friendly Oaks. Some remembered the balmy July day in 1922 when the trees, then mere seedlings, were dedicated and that stretch of Main Street was renamed Victory Avenue. They reminded people how Women's Club president Mrs. Frederick H. Guenther had spoken at the dedication, promising Sarasota's soldiers that their memorial was "an avenue of living trees, whose beauty and grateful shade would delight and bless generations long after you had passed on."

Soon the newspapers were full of the controversy. An editorial in The *News* on January 5, 1955 said, "We'd rather keep the oaks and let business plan to include them in its growth." But on January 7, The *News* reported, "First of Memorial Oaks Topples to Progress." The next day, under the bold headline "CITIZENS!!!" the Friends of Friendly Oaks placed an advertisement that asked, "Can the will of a few rob Sarasota of its heritage, its lovely avenue of shade trees? Will the center of Sarasota be left to broil in the blazing sun like a factory town?" A "Spare the Main Street Trees" coupon was enclosed to clip and mail to the organization to show support.

Prominent citizens joined the battle, among them Karl Bickel, former president of United Press who pointed out that such cosmopolitan cities as Paris and Rome

Main Street east from Orange Avenue was renamed Victory Avenue and lined with oaks to honor Sarasota's WWI servicemen. *Pete Esthus collection*

boasted shade trees. Children wrote letters of support. Bay Haven third grader Barbara Bell asked in her letter to the newspaper, "Why don't we give them water instead of killing them?" A petition brought twenty-five hundred signatures from Friends supporters. An expert from the University of Florida was called in and pronounced the trees healthy. He said removing them would be foolish. Maas Brothers president Jerome Waterman announced that ten oaks bordering the site of a recently proposed downtown Maas Brothers would be spared. (The *News* editorialized that in doing so he "earned the gratitude of the entire community.") An oak fronting the Texaco station was given a temporary stay. And an advisory committee was formed to deal with the "tree problem."

But protestations notwithstanding, the trees fell to progress, one by one. Today there is no mistaking Victory Avenue (Main Street) for a Rockwell painting. And if you stroll that stretch of concrete, you may wish that city leaders had heeded the Friends of Friendly Oaks and built around Mother Nature, not over her.

Pigskin Memories

BACK IN THE EARLY DAYS of football, when the T-formation was the most expeditious way to march the pigskin down the field, when noggins were protected with a full head of hair under a leather helmet, and noses not at all, a team of gridiron gladiators was formed called the Sarasota Salts.

It was 1947, two years after World War II, and the team was part of the newly formed Sarasota Veterans Athletic Association, a group of men who had missed the opportunity to compete in college or the pros because of the war.

They were sponsored by local merchants, who outfitted the team and paid their expenses until they could become self-sufficient through ticket sales. Former pro Dick Price coached.

These were the days before people could watch all sorts of pro and college teams on TV twenty-four hours a day seven days a week. Small cities like Sarasota followed their high school teams avidly. Sarasota High's Sailors were the pride of the county. The young players were truly local heroes, and Ihrig Field was packed on Friday nights with generations of fans screaming the team to victory.

For the most part, the Salts were grown-up Sarasota Sailors. The roster listed players that to this day are synonymous with the glory days of the orange and black: Joe Lovingood, Ellis Denham, the Bispham brothers, Jiggs Joyner, Randy Brooksbank and a host of others. Many would go on to make their mark upon our community. Salts quarterback Jack Betz, who became a city commissioner and Sarasota mayor, remembers them as a bunch of guys who just loved football. The hope was that the men's popularity would bring in the fans to see a rough-and-tumble brand of football somewhere between college and semipro. The program promised good ball: "The players are veterans of the recent war…and their record on the field of play is as exemplary and pre-eminent as their records on the field of battle."

Seven games were scheduled for the 1947 campaign, with the Salts working out at Payne Park in shorts and T-shirts. Their pads didn't arrive until the day of the opener against the Orlando Ramblers, a semipro team. Their helmets were borrowed from the high school.

What followed could have been expected of a team that didn't even have a real scrimmage behind them: a 41–0 drubbing. But after a week's practice, they held the Winter Haven VFW team to a 0–0 tie. Two losses followed, then one win and

Program for the mighty Sarasota Salts football team, 1948.

then a rematch with the Ramblers. The game was played at Ihrig Field, where for ninety cents the locals could watch the earlier loss be avenged. Even though three starters were out with broken ribs, the improved Salts managed a 0–0 tie. The season ended with a 14–0 victory over Winter Haven, highlighted by a double lateral and a thirty-five-yard pass from Betz to Jack Martin.

The Salts had a better year in 1948. The rules had been changed to allow anyone not attending school to play on the veterans team and the players had improved. Of the first five games, they lost only one and were poised to seize the state title. Only their nemesis, the Ramblers, stood in the way.

Two thousand showed up for the championship game, but the cheering couldn't carry the day. The Salts' half-time lead of 6–0 (a one-yard plunge by Lovingood after a forty-one-yard run by Martin) fell to 6–13 by the game's end. It was as close as the team would ever come.

The Salts continued to play ball into the 1950s before they hung up their cleats. They never won the championship, never, in fact, earned enough to pay the players anything but expenses. But money was not really the point. The point was that some boys who suddenly had to be men for the war got another shot at living a part of their youth that otherwise would have been lost.

That Sizzling Clarinetist

On December 28, 1940, Rudy Bundy, the man with the "sizzling clarinet," struck up his twelve-piece orchestra and became the star of Sarasota's nightlife.

His was the first big-name band to come to town since the Roaring Twenties, and the occasion that Saturday night was the formal opening of Sarasota's fabulous Lido Casino: "On Lido Beach, the Nights are Enchanting. It's Time to Listen to Rudy Bundy's Music…Borne on the Soft Gulf Breezes."

He was the contemporary of Benny Goodman, Glenn Miller (with whom he shared a manager), Artie Shaw and the Dorsey brothers. His band was a regular feature on CBS and the Mutual Broadcasting System, which carried music from popular nightclubs throughout the country to listeners coast to coast.

Dressed in sharply pressed tan slacks, brown double-breasted blazers and white-and-brown wingtips, his band members were a thrilling sight as they blasted out such swing-era hits as "Stompin' at the Savoy," "Begin the Beguine" and his personal favorite, "I'll Get By."

He lived until his death on Lido Key, in the distinctive home that his friend Detroit Tigers catcher Billy Sullivan designed for him in 1941. It's only a block away from the site of the former casino, accentuated by a boundary fence with the first five words to his theme song, "Thrill," carved in wood.

"Lots were going for four hundred dollars and five hundred dollars in those days," he told me. "And they weren't selling at that. Mosquitoes were so thick, you couldn't see outside the porch." He remembered paying the mosquito fogger an extra dollar to back the jeep onto the driveway and give the house a few extra blasts.

His den was a combination bar and museum. Black-framed photos filled the walls and went across the ceiling. They told the story of his career in music, a long stint as vice president of the Ringling Brothers and Barnum and Bailey Circus and friendships with decades of screen, sports and entertainment stars. Interspersed throughout were pictures of Bundy with his wife, Katie, and their family. A mantel carried a collection of autographed baseballs dating to Babe Ruth, and the bar was filled with glasses, ashtrays and swizzle sticks from world-famous nightclubs.

Bundy's first engagement in Sarasota was such a success that he stayed, built his first and only home and became an integral part of Sarasota's social scene. He

"The King of Sarasota Swing," Rudy Bundy, with his sizzling clarinet. *Rudy Bundy*

met John Ringling North at the Casino, and that friendship led to his association with the circus and to the opening of the M'Toto Room lounge in the then John Ringling Hotel (later the John Ringling Towers). The M'Toto Room opened in 1944, featuring Rudy Bundy and his band, and went on to become one of the most popular clubs in the city's history.

Bundy was on the board of directors of the Ringling Brothers circus for twenty years and was vice president and treasurer, a position he held because he had the trust of circus boss North. But he was never far from his clarinet, appearing often at the Lido Casino and playing clubs, lounges and parties around town into the late 1980s.

Rosemary Cemetery

In 1886, the Florida Mortgage and Investment Company, having promised much and delivered little, provided the space for a cemetery, and in 1903 it donated it to the small town of Sarasota. No money was set aside for its upkeep, a perennial problem that continues to this day.

In 1916 the Woman's Club published a plea for assistance in maintaining the cemetery in the *Sarasota Times*. Mrs. W.A. Grate, chairwoman of the cemetery committee, beseeched, "How many of our good people will send a dollar, or even fifty cents, or twenty-five, according to the condition of his or her purse?"

The same lack of funds has plagued most of the other groups that, over the years, have assumed responsibility for this hallowed plot of ground. In addition to the Woman's Club, they've included the Historical Society of Sarasota County, the Sarasota Alliance for Historic Preservation and friends and relatives of the deceased.

Located between Central Avenue and Florida Avenue, Rosemary Cemetery is named for the herb that denotes remembrance. Among the headstones are the names of citizens whose faith and hard work transformed Sarasota from yesterday's unknown backwater into today's inviting destination for visitors from around the world. Longtime Sarasota *Herald-Tribune* journalist Dorothy Stockbridge-Pratt once noted that the headstones read like the street names of Sarasota. Harry Higel is buried there, as are John Hamilton Gillespie, the town's first mayor; Owen Burns, who guided the city into the modern era; original colonists John Browning and his wife, Jane; the Reverend Lewis Colson and his wife, Irene, early leaders in the African American community (the only African Americans buried in the cemetery), and such locally well-known names as Stickney, Whitaker, Cunliff and others. To learn about them is to know the colorful history of the community.

Approximately 240 people of all ages and walks of life are buried beneath headstones made of granite, poured concrete, marble or brick and mortar; some of the headstones have become so weather-worn that they are no longer legible. Some have seashells embedded in them—one in the shape of a large heart. Others have badges, military insignias, pictures or holders of flames that have long since burned out.

Most touching are those with a small lamb, denoting that here lies a child. The inscriptions on two of them sum up the heartfelt sadness of them all: "From

A cleanup day at the cemetery. Proper maintenance is still a problem at the downtown landmark. *Sarasota County History Center*

mother's arms to the arms of Jesus" and, on the stone of four-year-old Robert Harold Gallagher, who died in 1930, "Darling We Miss You."

Some who died during the Great Depression when money was tight are buried without a marker. Others have epithets that amuse, such as Glenn Campbell Brye's "God does not deduct from man's allotted time those hours spent fishing." Dennis Joseph Brye's headstone reads like something out of *How to Win Friends and Influence People*. It says of him, "He was the man who dealt in sunshine and the one who won the crowds / He did a lot more business than the man who peddled clouds."

Perhaps the soul most at peace in the cemetery is that of W.A. Hodges, who is buried between his two wives. Then again, perhaps not.

Emilia Prime, who died in 1924, is remembered simply as "a good Christian." Heartbroken over the loss of their son, Paul Drymon, who died in 1912 at the age of seventeen, his parents had these comforting words etched on his stone: "No Pains, No Griefs, No Anxious Fear Can Reach Our Loved One Sleeping Here."

Centered in the cemetery is a stone pergola donated by Mrs. Palmer with seats "for the frequenters of this hollowed spot of rest." Mrs. Harry Higel donated a gate in 1911, with the reminder that it be closed so that cattle couldn't roam among the headstones and tear up the plants. Others donated shrubs, trees and fertilizer. In those days a plot cost from ten to twenty dollars.

In March 1887, Tom Booth, one of the colonists attracted to Sarasota by the promises of the Florida Mortgage and Investment Company, was the first to be buried in Rosemary Cemetery. His friends said that the worked himself to death. Later that year Elaf Green, a carpenter, went mad and murdered his wife and three young children. They, too, are buried there. He is not.

In 1915, the *Sarasota Times* quoted visiting professor W.B. Jones's praise of the cemetery, which he called "one of the most attractive and neatly kept cemeteries he had seen in Florida." Mostly, though, the cemetery has been in disrepair, with headstones damaged or in disarray and weeds grown everywhere; few flowers and much litter.

Recently a grant from the Mildred F. Doyle Trust through the Sarasota County Historical Society, with the assistance of Judy Ball and Deborah Dart, provided funds to repair some of the damaged markers and sponsor a cemetery conservation workshop to help volunteers care for the cemetery. Ball and Dart have also worked hard to have the cemetery protected by listing it with the National Trust for Historic Preservation. Perhaps in the near future the words on the stone of Henry F. Reils will ring true: "Here he lies where he longed to be."

Pretentious Palace

Although the local newspapers were frequently given to hyperbole and boasting during the effervescent years of the Roaring Twenties, the Sarasota *Herald*'s editorial assertion that Ringling's new home "is simply a forerunner of scores of splendid homes…which will grace the shoreline of our beautiful bay and magnificent gulf" turned out to have erred on the side of caution.

In fact, John and Mable Ringling's Ca' d'Zan became the forerunner of not scores, but hundreds of what have come to be known as trophy homes. And it remains the most inspiring and breathtaking of them all.

Abutting Sarasota Bay, the palatial mansion of the circus king, railway owner, oil prospector, art collector and, most importantly for Sarasota, developer was expressly built to be, as Mister John put it, "pretentious."

It's a storybook home, lavishly decorated and designed to show off and entertain highbrow guests, friends, relations and prospective Sarasota land buyers, a sample of the good life during the heady and excessive days of the Florida land boom. Jay Gatsby would have felt quite at home there. With only a little imagination, one can visualize an evening soiree on the marble-tiled terrace with glamorous guests sipping champagne and dancing the night away to jazz music. Within view across Sarasota Bay, not the East Egg of F. Scott Fitzgerald's novel, but Ringling's answer to the fine life that would be available on Longboat Key.

Through the Moorish-looking gatehouse, the long driveway to Ca' d'Zan is lined with palms, numerous antique statuary, urns, gigantic banyans, strands of bamboo, manicured shrubs, moss-covered oak trees and a gorgeous rose garden surrounded by more antique statues. In front of the home, which is set back nearly a quarter of a mile from Bay Shore Road, a walkway is guarded by two sphinxes. On the north side of the walk is a large marble swimming pool accentuated with colorful Spanish tiles. Across from it is a fountain with a statue of a young man pouring water from a jug. Between them is a mosaic compass inlaid with tiles and the signs of the zodiac. All very colorful.

The Ringlings were enamored with Europe, where they traveled frequently to vacation, scout for new circus acts and collect artwork. Venice was their favorite city, and into their home Mable wished to incorporate design features that were reminiscent of the Doge's Palace on the Grand Canal. To complete the sunny

Pretentious was the operative word. *Joseph Steinmetz collection. Sarasota County History Center*

The view from Sarasota Bay. *Joseph Steinmetz collection. Sarasota County History Center*

Venetian look, she even imported a gondola that was moored behind the mansion. (The gondola was wrecked during the hurricane of 1926.)

The commission for the reported million-dollar, thirty-two-room home was given to New York architect Dwight James Baum. No stranger to pleasing deep-pocketed customers, he worked closely with Mable, who had pictures and drawings of homes from abroad that interested her. Owen Burns was the builder. Mable also wished to incorporate a tower similar to the one Stanford White designed for Madison Square Garden, of which Ringling was a stockholder and where the Ringling Brothers and Barnum and Bailey Circus opened each year. At sixty-one feet tall, it offered an unsurpassed view; a light in it could be seen for miles around.

The project was started in 1925, when Sarasota was flush with optimism fueled by the rapidly rising real estate market and its get-rich potential. This was, after all, the Land of Glorified Opportunity.

It was reported that more than four hundred thousand dollars was spent on furnishings to outfit the home. Antiques, large paintings and colorful, intricately woven tapestry and rugs are everywhere. The ceiling in the ballroom was painted by renowned illustrator Willy Pogany and shows the dances of different nationalities. Music in the room was provided by an elegant Steinway piano. Another room features a huge Aeolian organ with hundreds of pipes that could be played electrically or manually. The Ringlings loved music, and the Czecho-Slovakian Band, brought to Sarasota by Ringling, gave recitals and concerts for Ringling parties.

By the time the mansion was completed, Sarasota's freewheeling days were numbered. The hurricane that blew away the gondola and the island near the home also blew out the flame of optimism that typified the era. Soon Ringling's fortune would be in jeopardy and so would his position as head of the circus. Worse, Mable, the love of his life, died in 1929. His marriage to Emily, dubious from the start, ended in a bitter divorce.

In 1936, John Ringling, cash strapped and weary of the perfidy of family members, former friends and business associates, died. To the people of the state of Florida, he left his art museum and Ca' d'Zan, the symbol of his and his community's success.

The Grandest Hotel of Them All

If there was a clue at the beginning of 1926 that the boom was nearly at an end, it was not apparent in the newspapers. Quite the contrary: throughout the year, the headlines and articles seemed to underscore the boastful assertion of the local chamber of commerce that "Sarasota's Growth Cannot Be Stopped."

In fact, however, the overweight lady was inching toward the microphone and was about to belt out, "The party's over!" It was nearly time to call it a day.

Even after the hurricane of September 18, 1926, which hit Miami with such dramatic force and burst the real estate bubble, Sarasota was still in a very Roaring Twenties, upbeat mood, full of itself as the El Vernona was nearing completion.

The formal opening was scheduled for December 31, 1926, with a New Year's celebration in the grand style, but the hotel was opened for public inspection on Labor Day and the Sarasota *Herald* bragged that the El Vernona was "one of the finest in Dixieland." It shared the front page with news of silent movie star Rudolph Valentino's funeral: "thousands pay homage...Pola Negri weeps."

The newspaper described Sarasota's newest and most luxurious hotel in detail, noting "the splendid view of beautiful Sarasota Bay" from most of the rooms. The construction cost was placed at more than $750,000 and it was prophesized that it would at once take its place as one of the leading inns in the entire nation. The public was told that this hotel was Sarasota's most pretentious—a word used often to describe Ca' d'Zan.

The dining room was a gargantuan fifty-two feet square with a skylight twenty-six feet high. Surrounded by massive columns and stenciled woodwork, the dining room was illuminated by "refulgent beams" of light from the crystal chandelier, which had formerly hung in the mansion of John Jacob Astor and "had for eons gazed upon stately dames and budding debutantes." A lovely Spanish fountain was centered under the skylight, and it was said that colored shafts of light played on the splashing water at night, creating a mystic effect.

The El Vernona was to be operated by Harry Griswold, "an experienced hotel man and well known with years of experience as his asset." He had been recommended by Ringling as a "personal friend who was one of our best hotel men." Griswold was said to have been in the hotel business for twenty-five years and contracted to lease the El Vernona for five years at fifty thousand dollars per

Situated on Sarasota Bay on what was then called Broadway Avenue, the El Vernona Hotel and adjacent Burns office, which became the Karl Bickel House. In the center of this picture are the Frances-Carlton Apartments. *Sarasota County History Center*

year plus two hundred dollars per month for each of the shops that occupied the front of the building. The choice of Griswold would prove to be as unfortunate for Burns as was the timing of the hotel's construction.

As the date for the grand opening drew near despite the multitude of problems and last-minute details associated with such a large project, neither the choice of his manager nor the poor timing of the hotel's construction was on Burns's mind.

As Burns was the builder of Ringling's mansion, he collaborated with Ca' d'Zan architect Dwight James Baum, and they developed a positive working relationship. Baum located his office on the second floor of Burns's office building (known later as the Bickel House), and the two teamed up to produce some of Sarasota's loveliest homes and commercial buildings. The Sarasota *Herald* praised their efforts in a story: "Dwight Baum and Burns in Boon to City," noting that the three homes they built on St. Armand's Key "have set the pace that will make this palm covered key the most delightful residential community within the environs of Sarasota." The two also worked together on the Pineapple Apartments at Herald Square.

Baum's design of the El Vernona was called "a reproduction of a medieval palace of the Dons." It was accentuated throughout with numerous antiques, colorfully painted tiles from Spain and Tunis, massive cypress beams stenciled with playfully fighting lions and ornate wrought iron chandeliers, candleholders and hanging lanterns. The three-hundred-year-old roof tiles were imported from homes and buildings in Granada. Taken all together, the effect was said to be as truly Spanish as anything outside of Spain could ever hope to be.

In the reading room hung fine paintings, some of which came from the collection of John Jacob Astor.

A winding stone stairway led to a lovely arcaded piazza on the second floor, which contained a roof garden with a fountain and enough open space for dancing or lounging with friends. Facing the highway, the piazza was located in the area between the two main parts of the building and was protected by a long red-tiled colonnade of eight tall arches.

Two rooftop penthouse bungalows—"marvels of design, convenience and furnishing"—were placed to add symmetry to the building's large observation tower and were richly outfitted as was a special rooftop suite of rooms with a private porch. The hotel contained seventy-two thousand square feet of space, and the work was so detailed that even screws were antiquated and had to be of a particular type.

All of the 150 rooms in the six-story building offered running ice water and steam heat. Each room was furnished with twin beds, wicker chaise, table with telephone and lamp, rattan floor lamp, wicker chair and overhead lamp. The floors were checkerboard tiles. Larger suites offered a sofa, comfortable stuffed chairs and extra tables.

As one would expect in a hotel that claimed to be one of the finest in the South, epicurean meals were served. The staff of chefs was led by Bourgilett Boyer, "chef deluxe," whose years of culinary craftsmanship had taken him to the most famous hotels in America and Europe. He was paid ten thousand dollars per year, no small sum in the 1920s, especially since the hotel was opened for only a seasonal three months each year.

No expense was spared outfitting Bourgilett's kitchen, which was given a 100 percent rating from the state hotel department with the inspector noting, "In fact the hotel has gone even far beyond our requirements in the way of providing safety for its patrons in the matter of food and comfort."

Service was unexcelled. Patrons were pampered. Guests were promised that the courtesy one expected in the wayside inns of Andalusia was an eternal command of every El Vernona employee.

Entertainment included concerts, recitals, dances, tea parties and ritzy balls. The ever present Czecho-Slovakian National Banvd played there. During National Music Week, Miss Marie Navelle, "the greatest woman pianist of the time," played, accompanied by her violinist, Haydon Gunther. In these days before political correctness, a music critic commented, "[He] was the only good thing to come out of Mexico."

Diners listened to the El Vernona Orchestra in the room "where fountains play—and soft music fills the air." The dance floor was made of highly polished maple and the goings-on could be viewed from the skylight.

Each week, the hotel's guests and the names of their hometowns were listed in the local papers, which also detailed the special events put on for out-of-towners and local society: "Mrs. G.W. Matthews of Dallas, Texas was the honored guest at a delightful bridge luncheon given at the El Vernona Hotel...The table was effectively decorated and a sumptuous four course luncheon was served the guests." Another: "In the softly lighted reception rooms of the El Vernona yesterday afternoon, society met at one of the loveliest affairs given this season, a formal matinee by Mrs. Walter R. Miller, Mrs. Jo Gill, and Miss Ruth Truesdell."

Whatever the occasion, the participants were invariably given high praise: "Mrs. Landess was beautiful in rose chiffon. Mrs. Caples was lovely as always in a frock of orchid chiffon, with fuchsia cape and deep orchid velvet slippers. Mrs. Guenther, pouring, held herself with majestic dignity becoming her lovely grey hair, set off with a beautiful strand of pearls roped around her throat, and soft blue gown."

The New Year's opening celebration was the climax of the local real estate boom. As he sat beside his lovely wife, Vernona, at the table of honor in her namesake hotel, awash in the glow of the toasts and plaudits of their contemporaries, Burns, at the pinnacle of his success, had every reason to believe that the future would continue to be as bright as 1926 rolled into 1927. At the stroke of midnight, "the din that rose from the scene of this merrymaking was nothing short of deafening."

Trouble was approaching quickly, however. According to Lillian Burns, manager Griswold bolted town, leaving a hotel filled with guests. He had paid nothing on his lease agreement and was not heard from again. By way of explanation of his departure, the newspaper indicated that he was required to go north for treatment. The malady was not specified. This was a major blow to Burns, who had counted on the lease money as well as Griswold's management skills.

Owen Burns III, Burns' nephew, was quickly pressed into service and guided the El Vernona through the remainder of the first season. Described as "a popular young man about town," he was eager to be successful. When the hotel closed for the season, he attended Cornell University, taking courses in hotel management to prepare for the next season.

The 1927–28 season opener was only slightly less glamorous that the grand opening celebration and was given ample press coverage. Owen Burns and Owen Burns III put up a solid front, with Burns III informing the paper that business was better than ever. "Lest there be any impression existing that the city is not receiving the tourist business this year, I should like to say that the El Vernona—and I assume this is true of the other places—is entertaining more winter visitors than ever before in its history."

It would be the hotel's last hurrah under Burns's ownership and management. By the end of 1928 the local economy slowed dramatically. An editorial in the

Inside the ballroom of the El Vernona after it had been transformed into the John Ringling Hotel, is Captain Heyer atop his magnificent Starless Night. John Ringling North imbued the hotel with the atmosphere of the circus, and for many years the hotel was managed by Charles Carr Sr. This show is being put on as a fund-raiser for St. Martha's Church. *Helen Griffin collection. Sarasota County History Center*

Sarasota *Herald* on November 27, 1928 explained to its readers, "Florida has had a wild rush of settlers. It is now in the process of bringing order out of chaos."

Sarasota's real estate doldrums were exacerbated by the financial crash of Wall Street in October 1929 and the ensuing depression. For Burns and his generation of developers and town builders, the men who took the canvas of Sarasota and painted upon it one of the most beautiful communities in the nation, the heady days were over and foreclosures and bankruptcies replaced building permits and grand openings.

On December 1, 1930 the Sarasota *Herald* informed readers, "El Vernona Hotel Sold To N.Y. Firm." The paper reported that the Prudence Bond Company had foreclosed on the hotel. The furnishings were sold back to the John Wanamaker Company of New York for fifty thousand dollars. Attorneys said that the hotel would be reopened the coming year.

Shortly thereafter, John Ringling acquired the hotel, thus ending one chapter and beginning another for a hotel christened the Aristocrat of Beauty.

Miscellany

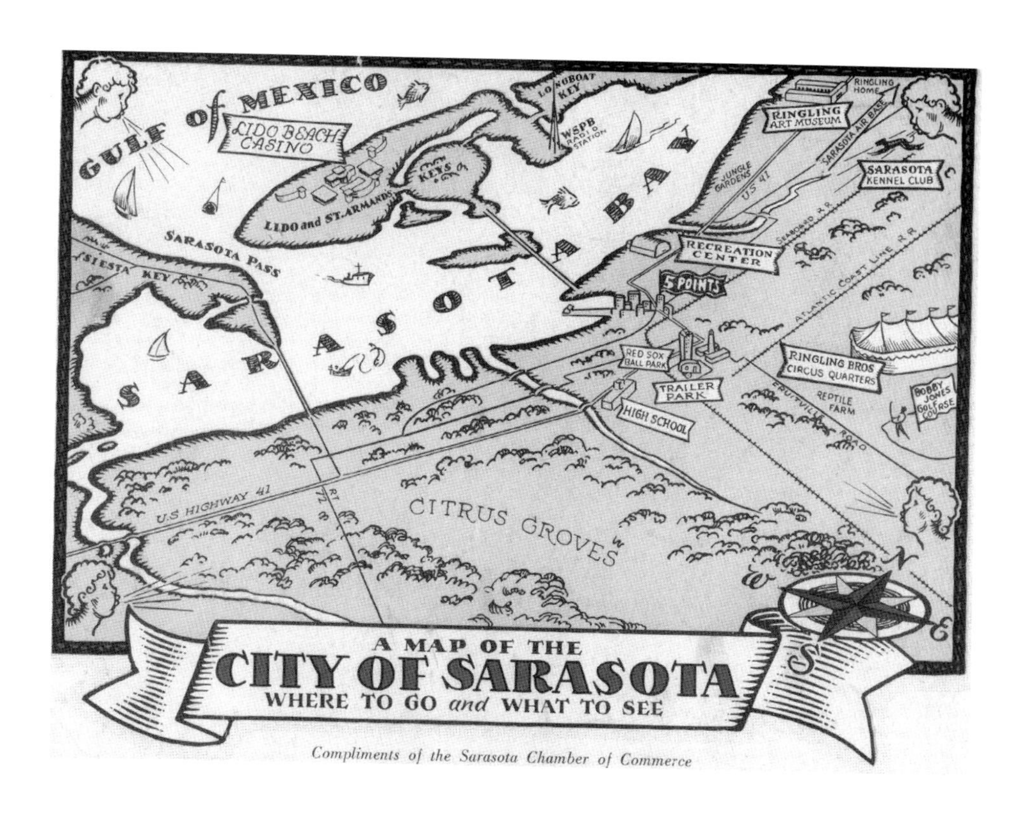

"WHERE TO GO and WHAT TO SEE" in Sarasota in the 1930s, '40s and '50s. The biggest attraction was the Ringling Brothers Circus Quarters, which was the most popular tourist attraction in the state until Disney World opened in Orlando. Note the large portion on the map devoted to "Citrus Groves." The development of South Gate, built near this area, would later advertise itself as "Where You Live Among the Orange Blossoms."

Vernona Freeman on the day of her marriage to Owen Burns, June 4, 1912. The couple married in New York City in what was described as "one of the prettiest weddings of this month." After the ceremony, they were off for a three-month tour of Europe. When they returned to Sarasota, the town's brass band met them at the train station and they were serenaded to their home for ice cream, cake and punch. Owen, Sarasota's first major developer, arrived in Sarasota in 1910 and bought out the holdings of the Florida Mortgage and Investment Company and at once became the owner of approximately 75 percent of what would become the city of Sarasota. It was for Vernona that his fabulous hotel, apartment building and Vernona Avenue were named. The couple would stay happily married until Owen's death in 1937. They had five children. Vernona died on Christmas Eve in 1974. *Lillian Burns*

Owen Burns aboard ship on his way to his European honeymoon with Vernona. Owen and Vernona met when she came to Sarasota with relatives for a visit. The *Sarasota Times* reported, "The young lady visited at Burns Villa this past winter, and was a general favorite among Sarasota's younger set." He fell in love with her at first sight and when she left to return home, Burns unexpectedly boarded the train with her and her entourage. Shortly thereafter he announced his intentions to ask for her hand and after a brief courtship, he proposed to her while having tea at the Ritz-Carlton in New York. *Lillian Burns*

Outfitted in their summer uniforms, these letter carriers are standing in front of the Sarasota Post Office, which had been dedicated by U.S. postmaster James A. Farley in 1935. The building, preserved by the city, now houses city offices as well as a space for the Sarasota Historical Society. *A. Richard Baron*

Graduates of what was billed as the World's Only Shell Class. In this 1937 picture, the ladies show their support for Franklin Roosevelt's Works Progress Administration program while proudly displaying art in shells. A few have their home state noted: South Dakota, Connecticut, Virginia and Iowa can be seen. Sarasota benefited mightily from the WPA during the Great Depression with projects such as Bayfront Park and the Municipal Auditorium, the Lido Casino and the Sarasota-Bradenton Airport. This picture was taken on a pier at Lido Beach that extended over the sand to the gulf. Today the pier would be shorter, much shorter. *Sarasota County History Center*

Standing proudly on the steps of the Sarasota courthouse, wearing Sam Browne belts and shiny badges, these young men are members of Sarasota's first School Boy Patrol, circa 1926. Behind them from the left: name unknown, state organizer; Chief of Police S. Tilden Davis; Mayor E.J. Bacon and Professor T.W. Yarborough of Sarasota High School. Yarborough was appointed superintendent of Sarasota County Public Schools in 1921, a position he held until 1944. During his twenty-three-year tenure, he handed out the diplomas to every graduating senior at Sarasota High School. *Sarasota County History Center*

Sarasota School Board president Philip Hiss and architects of what came to be known as the Sarasota School of Architecture. These men and others not pictured put Sarasota on the international map with their modern designs that "brought the outside in." *Courtesy Sarasota County History Center* from the book *Sarasota School of Architecture* by John Howey

OFFICIAL BALLOT

CITY OF SARASOTA

Sarasota, Florida

SPECIAL ELECTION FOR BONDS

Tuesday, September 5th, A. D., 1916

Make a cross mark (X) before the word of your choice.

For authorizing purchase of real estate for park purposes and issuing bonds therefor.

	Yes
	No

For construction of Municipal Pier and issuing bonds therefor.

	Yes
	No

The ballot of 1916. No chads—hanging, bulging, dimpled or pregnant. And if a recount were necessary, it wouldn't have taken long—fewer than a hundred *X*s to count. Voted down in this official ballot was the purchase of real estate for park purposes—a golf course. The pier proposition carried, making Sarasota one of only two cities in the state that owned a pier; St. Petersburg was the other. The vote for the pier was forty-five in favor, twenty-nine against. For the golf links, thirty-five in favor, forty-two against. The *Sarasota Times* noted, "It is too bad that all could not see the necessity of having a golf course here." The local sentiment regarding golf courses has since changed. *Sarasota County History Center*

Taken on June 8, 1925, the back of this photograph is inscribed: "Mr. Owen Burns, These are the roofs from which your tiles are coming from Granada. This picture was taken on the Alhambra hill, right under the Vermillion Towers. (Signed) C.F. Wickes." The tiles would be used for the El Vernona Hotel and other of Burns's many construction projects in Sarasota. *Lillian Burns*

The first bridge to Siesta Key, Sarasota Key then, was erected in 1917, and finally one of Sarasota's beautiful beaches was accessible by car. In those days the cars were mostly Fords and mostly black. The bridge was replaced in 1927 by another narrow span that served until the 1970s. Mrs. V. D. Jones, bridge tender there for more than twenty years, served eighteen of those years twenty-four hours a day, seven days a week. Her home there consisted of a kitchen (which also housed the bridge controls), bedroom and bath. She told a *Herald-Tribune* reporter that she had been off twice in her twenty years, once to have an operation and once to attend the funeral services of her husband. *Sarasota County History Center*

The Sarasota Minstrels group was organized by Dr. Jack Halton (to the left in the open coat). Halton was an eye, ear, nose and throat specialist who had a grand baritone voice. He moved to Sarasota in 1905, opened the Halton Sanitarium, managed the Desoto Hotel, served one term as councilman and in 1932 received the American Legion community service award for his work with underprivileged children. He died in 1942 doing what he loved, singing, at a convention in St. Petersburg. This picture was taken in 1916 at Five Points. *Sarasota County History Center*

Fire Chief Henry Behrens (steering) sits atop the city of Sarasota's new Armstrong LaFrance fire truck on South Pineapple Avenue, 1915. The building in the background is the Sarasota Bank, today the site of Patrick's Restaurant and Tavern. Behrens was chosen as the first fire chief in 1908, having served as chief of the volunteer fire department. He was paid seventy-five dollars per month. This fire engine cost almost nine thousand dollars, could pump 750 gallons of water a minute and could shoot a stream of water 120 feet high. On the community's few paved streets, it could hit sixty miles per hour. (Its replacement fire engine, purchased in 1928, was repossessed in 1932 during the Great Depression.) When Behrens left the fire department in 1921, he turned his talents to being a gunsmith and designed and produced some remarkable weapons. He died in 1967 at age eighty-four. *Sarasota County History Center*

Opened in 1912, the all-brick thirty-eight-room Palms Hotel was located in the three-story Tonnelier Building on the north side of lower Main Street near Five Points. The modern building also housed the Palms Theatre, Dr. Joseph Halton's medical office, the Crescent Pharmacy, the New York Store and a barber shop, a bakery and a fruit stand. Declared fireproof, it burned to the ground in a spectacular hundred-thousand-dollar fire on March 8, 1915, taking all the businesses and their contents with it. Sarasota's new Armstrong LaFrance fire engine arrived the next month. *Sarasota County History Center*

The Sarasota Brass Band marches proudly along upper Main Street, carrying the stars and stripes in this 1918 photograph. Note the "Welcome Buddies" sign painted on the street to greet returning doughboys who had gone over there to battle the Kaiser's army in 1917. The flagpole was erected at the center of Five Points in their honor. In 1928, the American Legion War Memorial would be dedicated at this site, where it would remain until 1954. Another honor for the returning servicemen was the renaming of Main Street, east from Orange Avenue, as Victory Avenue and the planting of oak trees along the way, one for each Sarasota soldier. *Sarasota County History Center*

Looking south along Gulf Stream Avenue, during the mid-1950s at a time when downtown Sarasota and its crown jewel, Sarasota Bay, were still linked. To the right is City Hall in the Hover Arcade and City Pier. To the left center is the Palmer Bank, for many years Sarasota's flagship bank. The other tall buildings are the Sarasota Hotel and the Orange Blossom Hotel. In City Planner John Nolen's comprehensive plan for Sarasota, a 1925 aerial photograph of the bay front was included with the caption "The attractiveness of this spot drew the original settlers, and today is still the city's greatest asset." *Sarasota County History Center*

Presto. Suddenly, downtown and the bay are worlds apart—at least four lanes, speeding traffic, traffic islands, and a parking lot apart—never to be reconnected. This 1960s aerial shot shows U.S. 41 after it was rerouted in front of Gulf Stream Avenue. Still standing in the left center of the picture is the old city hall, soon to be declared a useless eyesore and demolished in the late '60s. In April 1958 at a symposium of architects hosted by renowned architect Paul Rudolph, participant Douglas Haskell, editor of the *Architectural Form*, slammed Bay Front Drive. Not bothering to mince words, he was quoted as saying, "It's a filthy dirty crime. It's unforgivable and idiotic, cutting off the community (from the bay front)." He went on, "I declare that gorillas, chimpanzees, dogs, monkeys and jackasses could not do worse than they have done to Sarasota." When former city manager Ross Windom returned to town and saw the bay front, he said, "A first class specialist must have designed the drive according to his own wishes, completely mutilating it." *Sarasota County History Center*

The Belle Haven Inn was Sarasota's first real hotel—for a time the community's pride and joy. Constructed by John Hamilton Gillespie of the Florida Mortgage and Investment Company as the DeSoto Hotel, it opened with grand fanfare on February 25, 1887. (According to Grismer in *The Story of Sarasota*, many of the men who attended didn't sober up for two days.) But by 1910, when Bertha Palmer and her entourage came to Sarasota for a look-see, the hotel was in such poor condition that Mrs. Palmer had to be put up in the Halton Sanitarium, refurnished for her visit. The hotel was later spruced up and expanded. In the mid-1920s it was demolished to make way for the American National Bank, later the Orange Blossom Hotel. *Sarasota County History Center*

Opened in 1968, Ben Stahl's Museum of the Cross was built to showcase his masterpieces, the Fourteen Stations of the Cross plus the Resurrection. Stahl was a world-renowned artist, illustrator and author. Among the fifty awards he won for his artwork was the Saltus Gold Medal from the National Academy of Design.

One of Sarasota's lingering mysteries is who broke into the Museum of the Cross one night in April 1969 and stole all fifteen of the massive paintings, then valued at more than a million dollars and not insured.

The loss hurt Stahl financially. He and his wife moved to Mexico for a time, then returned to Sarasota, where he died in 1987. The paintings have never been recovered. *Sarasota County History Center*

Sarasota, 1954. When longtime residents wax nostalgic about yesterday's Sarasota, the shops and stores in this shot of Main Street, looking toward the bay, illustrate the places they think of. The awning at the far left is in front of Badger's Drugs, "the Store of the Town." Along the way is Harmon's, Sears, Sal's Pizza (Sal was credited with bringing pizza to Sarasota and was billed as "the Pizza King"), Lois Lee and the Orange Blossom Hotel. Across the street, the popular Sport Shop, "For Sportswear and Everywhere," Bacchus Liquors, the Blossom Shop, Johnny's Coffee Shop, Hotel Sarasota, the Colonial Hotel and at the end of the street the archway at City Hall and onto the pier. If time could have stood still for Sarasota, this would have been a good time to do it. *E.E. Moore. Sarasota County History Center*

Some of Hollywood's most popular stars came to Sarasota for six weeks in 1951 to film Cecil B. DeMille's *The Greatest Show on Earth*. The community was wowed by the celebrities, who included the blond bombshell Betty Hutton, Dorothy Lamour (known as the "Bond Bombshell" during World War II for selling millions of dollars of war bonds), Charlton Heston, Cornel Wilde and Gloria Grahame. The world premiere was at Sarasota's Florida Theatre. The film went on to win Oscars for best picture and best story. Many locals had bit parts in the movie. *Pete Esthus*

"Mack" McDonald opened the Smack in 1934 in what had been the Ducky Wucky hamburger stand on the corner of Main and Pine Streets. The sign reads, "After dark please flash your lights for service. We will appreciate your cooperation in keeping down noise." In 1937 Smack's moved to Main Street and Osprey Avenue, where it became one of Sarasota's favorite gathering places. The building in the background is Central Elementary School, which closed in 1962, replaced by the post office. *Sarasota County History Center*

The Smack at Main Street and Osprey Avenue, as most longtime Sarasotans remember it. *Sarasota County History Center*

Owners Raymond Fernandez, Randy Hagerman and Benny Alvarez along with staff and family members gather at the Plaza to celebrate Christmas. Fine food, friendly service and a great bar characterized the Plaza, making it the focal point of downtown Sarasota—a gathering place for writers, artists, politicians, businesspeople, locals and tourists out for a good time. The third gentleman from the right in the sport coat is the bartender Joe Mitchell, known as "Flash." He remembered each regular's drink and would often have it poured and waiting before he or she sat down. *Sarasota County History Center*

Funded by John Tuttle Chidsey and opened in 1941, the Chidsey Library was designed by the prolific architectural firm Thomas Reed Martin Studios. Today this is the Sarasota County History Center at 701 North Tamiami Trail and houses a vast collection of data and photographs important to the county's history. Many of the photographs for my books came from the history center.

Embedded in the beautiful terrazzo floor in front of the checkout desk is a compass.

The site of the library and the adjacent Bayfront Park and Municipal Auditorium were obtained by the city for fifteen thousand dollars in tax certificates from the failed Sarasota Bay Hotel Company, which did not survive the Great Depression. The Chidsey building was used as a library until August 1976, when the Selby Public Library opened. *Sarasota County History Center*

Part of the annual Sara de Sota pageant, sponsored by the junior chamber of commerce, included a stint in the monkey cage on Main Street near Five Points. In the slammer in this 1948 picture is Johnny Roventini, whose stage name was Johnny Philip Morris. All of four feet tall, he was famous for his "Call for Philip MMMMMoooorrrrriiiiiissssss." The weeklong pageant with its grand parade was the highlight of the season and drew tens of thousands of spectators each year to one of the largest celebrations of its kind in the country. The Royal Court that year included Gordon Brye, Albert McFadyen, Bill Summerall, Jack Betz, Herschel House, Earlene Philpot, Lois Robbins, Joanne Quinn, Lucyle Chenney and Harriet Sturgis. *Sarasota County History Center*

Quintessential Sarasota? There was the ambiance, of course; the slow pace and the friendly locals who all seemed to know each other; the natural beauty of the beaches and the bay. Downtown had not yet been mucked up by overdevelopment—and there was the Lido Casino in all its beachfront glory. A place to dine, dance, drink, shop and just sit and watch. It stood for only twenty-nine years, and if the dream of most locals could come true, their Lido Casino would come back. *Sarasota County History Center*

The 1950s were heady times for Sarasota. Postwar optimism was running high and *progress* and *modern* were the catchwords of the day. The newspapers were full of grand openings, full-page advertisements for new subdivisions and headcounts of tourists and new residents. Editorials predicted little Sarasota was on the verge of becoming a grown-up city, an assertion underscored by the installation of new fluorescent lights that provided a "White Way" for downtown Sarasota. On October 26, 1954, the whole town celebrated its new lights—and new sophistication—with the Jubilee of Light Festival. *Sarasota County History Center*

A whirl of light around the American Legion War Memorial at Five Points and east along upper Main Street. To the left are the Palmer Bank, Lord's Arcade, the Ritz Theatre, and the DeSoto Hotel. To the right, Liggett's Drugs (later Madison's Drugs, and today Patrick's Restaurant and Tavern), the Kress Building and the small shops that made up downtown in the 1940s. The war memorial was deemed a traffic hazard in 1954, and over the protestations of many, it was moved to Gulf Stream Avenue, where it couldn't jump out at traffic. *Carmen Ramsey collection. Sarasota County History Center*

About the Author

JEFF LAHURD IS THE HISTORY specialist for Sarasota County. He and his wife, Jennifer, have four children and two grandchildren. Jeff grew up in Sarasota and attended school at St. Martha's, Cardinal Mooney and Sarasota High. He has a BA and an MA from the University of South Florida. He has written a history column for *Sarasota Magazine* for fifteen years and is a contributor to many local publications. His video, *Sarasota: Landmarks of the Past,* was shown on the History Channel and won an award from the Florida Trust for Historic Preservation for outstanding contribution to preservation in the field of communication.